Building Coalitions

Total Quality Education for the World's Best Schools

The Comprehensive Planning and Implementation Guide for School Administrators

Series Editor: **Larry E. Frase**

The authors dedicate this series to the memory of
W. Edwards Deming, 1900-1993

Building Coalitions

How to Link TQE Schools With Government, Business, and Community

Betty E. Steffy
Jane Clark Lindle

CORWIN PRESS, INC.
A Sage Publications Company
Thousand Oaks, California

For information address:

Corwin Press, Inc.
A Sage Publications Company
2455 Teller Road
Thousand Oaks, California 91320

SAGE Publications Ltd.
6 Bonhill Street
London EC2A 4PU
United Kingdom

SAGE Publications India Pvt. Ltd.
M-32 Market
Greater Kailash I
New Delhi 110 048 India

Printed in the United States of America

Library of Congress Cataloging-in-Publication Data

Steffy, Betty E.
  Building coalitions : how to link TQE schools with government, business, and community / authors, Betty E. Steffy, Jane Clark Lindle.
    p. cm. — (Total quality education for the world's best schools ; v. 5)
  Includes bibliographical references.
  ISBN 0-8039-6105-7 (pbk.: alk. paper)
  1. School management and organization—United States.
2. Education—United States—Aims and objectives. 3. Community and school—United States. 4. Total quality management—United States.
5. Coalition (Social sciences) I. Lindle, Jane Clark. II. Title.
III. Series.
LB2805.S7455   1994
371.2'00973—dc20   93-47954

94 95 96 97 98 10 9 8 7 6 5 4 3 2 1

Corwin Production Editor: Yvonne Könneker

Contents

Foreword

This book comes at a most opportune time. Of the many challenges facing public schools today, possibly the greatest entail the rapidly expanding duties and responsibilities assigned to schools. Every public school administrator has experienced the exasperation of facing virtually unlimited community and government "wants" with diminishing resources. From its inception, public education has been confronted with a growing list of responsibilities. The growth has been cumulative, and the pace is increasing appreciably. Schools are not now, nor have they ever been, able to do everything needed for America's youth by curing society's ills. Society's problems were created by society and belong to society, not education. Their resolution is the responsibility of society, of which education is a part.

Professors Steffy and Lindle have built and nurtured coalitions at all levels: school, school district, state department of education, and university. The Kentucky Education Reform Agenda owes much of its success to their leadership and expertise at the design, implementation, and monitoring stages.

Betty Steffy has served as a director of curriculum, assistant superintendent, and superintendent. She has authored numerous professional articles and books. *Career Stages of Classroom Teachers* (1989) and her most recent book, *The Kentucky Education Reform: Lessons for America* (1993), have enjoyed extensive circulation. She also serves as a consultant to many school districts and departments of education. Jane Lindle has served as regular and special education teacher and principal in Wisconsin. She completed a study of the

Kentucky School Councils program to determine how parents and community members are involved in school-based decision making and council members' satisfaction with communication within the councils. She has worked extensively with family resource and youth service centers in Kentucky and is currently writing a book titled *Micro-Political Problems of Leadership.*

Steffy and Lindle have combined their rich experience and expertise to offer a dynamic, no-nonsense book that gives educators the tools and strategies for conceptualizing, designing, and implementing coalitions. Combining the forces of the schools, the lay community, businesses, and social service organizations is crucial to a successful attack on the ever-growing list of societal problems and to educating America's youth. This book will be invaluable to educators at all levels, particularly principals and superintendents. With this book, they can gain the knowledge, tools, and techniques they need to increase the power of their education systems through coalitions.

Larry E. Frase
San Diego State University

Preface

The theme of this book is the valuing of children to construct high-quality communities. Many communities have become silent or have forgotten about the value of children. In the interest of "doing business," communities often have very short-term orientations to children and their problems and needs. Because child care and education consume community resources with few short-term paybacks, some have devalued children and labeled those who care for them *nonproductive.*

Total Quality Management (TQM) promotes a more long-term, strategic look at organizations; by extension, Total Quality Education (TQE) promotes an essential, strategic view of our communities, educational provisions, and ultimately our children. TQM has served to reorient business to focus less on the immediate bottom line and more on long-term quality. This book discusses extending that reorientation to a TQE, communitywide focus.

Some communities will have to be reminded that their children are their future. Some schools will have to be reminded that they serve more than children and parents; they also serve communities, businesses, and government. We refer to students and their parents as the primary clientele of schools; businesses, communities, and government form schools' secondary clientele. Refocusing communities on schools and schools on their communities is at the heart of TQE. Revaluing children and the schools that serve them will amount to a major campaign.

We have designed this book to help readers organize such a campaign for their communities. In the following chapters, we offer practical tips, checklists, charts, reflective forms for developing strategies, surveys for data collection, and information management tactics. We also include examples from communities and schools in the "real world" who are thinking more strategically by investing in children and their education. These investments take the form of more than simple monetary gifts, more than recycling cast-off company equipment, more than publicity stunts with short-term payoffs. The examples we discuss come from long-term projects with high-touch, personal involvement of business, government, and communities in schools.

All of the 14 principles espoused by W. Edwards Deming for TQM are relevant to this task. We will refer to them throughout the book. We present them here in Table 1, codified in a matrix that delineates TQE principles for both primary and secondary clientele of schools.

We can think of no more important task before us than to ensure the efficacy of the nation's public schools and to engage in and to resolve the issue of quality. But, as we make clear in this book, *it cannot be done alone!* Schools must have partners to be successful. It is to this working partnership that we now turn.

Betty E. Steffy
Jane Clark Lindle
University of Kentucky

TABLE 1. How Deming's 14 Points Relate to the Clientele of Schools

Point	Primary Clients (Students and Parents)	Secondary Clients (Government, Business, and Community)
1. Establish constancy of purpose for continuous improvement.	Schools empower students and parents to increase capacity for learning. Schools continually seek means of increasing student and parental commitment to high student performance.	Schools solicit involvement from government, businesses, and community to set standards for school/student outcomes; supplement school/parent capacities for supporting student achievement; provide cohesive commitment to achievement of school outcomes.
2. Adopt the new philosophy.	Schools solicit student input and parental perceptions. Schools solve problems by including students and parents in decision making. Schools encourage student ideas and address parental criticism.	Schools seek and accept expertise or insights from government, businesses, and community in identifying and addressing issues.
3. Cease dependence on mass inspection; build in quality.	Schools seek parental and student input at the beginning of a course of study. Parents' insights on student behavior and learning are most useful before problems arise. Students are empowered to monitor and evaluate their learning and progress toward outcomes. Parents and educators work together in helping students develop individual initiative and intrinsic motivation.	Schools provide government, businesses, and community with midcourse indicators of success and performance. Schools work with government, businesses, and community in providing real-world experiences outside the classroom. Schools utilize resources of government, businesses, and community in educative activities.

TABLE 1. Continued

Point	Primary Clients (Students and Parents)	Secondary Clients (Government, Business, and Community)
4. End the practice of doing business on price tag alone.	Schools collaborate with students and parents by honoring individual talents as opposed to labeling deficits. Schools adapt to the changing needs of families.	Schools provide the necessary information for enabling government, businesses, and community to address changing student and parental needs.
5. Improve constantly and forever.	Mistakes and failures are honored as important steps to achievement. Students and parents are empowered to diagnose and provide solutions to their own problems.	Schools provide learning opportunities for government, businesses, and community about human growth, development, and learning capacities.
6. Institute programs of experiential/on-the-job training.	Schools offer chances for students to experience a variety of opportunities. Schools monitor parental needs and provide necessary training.	Schools apprise and collaborate with government, businesses, and community in addressing training needs.
7. Institute leadership.	Schools provide settings for students and parents to develop leadership skills. School personnel develop a culture that nurtures one another's learning as well as incorporates students and parents as part of the learning community.	Schools set a helping agenda to solicit constructive leadership in collaboration with government, businesses, and community.
8. Drive out fear.	Schools provide opportunities for increasing parents' and students' self-esteem. Schools resist adopting defensive approaches to addressing parental and student concerns.	Schools drop competitive approaches in consulting with government, businesses, and community. Schools promote constructive approaches to addressing educational and social issues.

9. Break down barriers between staff areas.	Schools offer nonthreatening opportunities for conversations with students and parents. School staff are encouraged to sacrifice status-enhancing behavior for increased communication and capacity for student achievement with students and parents.	Schools encourage government, businesses, and community to establish multigroup design teams to address local educational and social concerns.
10. Eliminate slogans, exhortations, and targets.	Schools, parents, and students equitably share power, responsibility, and rewards for achieving outcomes.	Schools engage government, businesses, and community in productive solving of educational and social issues rather than competitive displays of blame fixing.
11. Eliminate numerical quotas.	Schools help students set performance standards rather than have them compete for letter grades or test scores. Schools help parents understand the benefit of goals and standards over grades and tests.	Schools engage government, businesses, and community in discourse about meaningful standards for schooling rather than grades and test scores.
12. Remove barriers to pride and joy of workmanship.	Learning is fun. Schools guard students from the cultural tendency to take work too seriously. Schools nurture parents' view of learning to be supportive of challenging yet enjoyable tasks.	Schools commission government, businesses, and community to provide pleasant settings and materials for encouraging student learning. Schools seek government, business, and community involvement in establishing school settings as a source of pride.
13. Institute a vigorous program of education and self-improvement.	Schools extend educational activities beyond students to parents and extended families.	Schools include government, businesses, and community in the reinvention of schools as communities of learning.
14. Put everyone to work on the transformation.	Schools immerse students and parents in opportunities to begin implementing TQE points.	Schools arrange meaningful events for government, businesses, and community to address the 14 points.

✧   ✧

About the Authors

Betty E. Steffy, Ed.D., is formerly the Deputy Superintendent of Instruction in the Kentucky Department of Education, as well as Superintendent of Schools in New Jersey and Assistant Superintendent of Schools in New York. She is the author or coauthor of four books, the latest two being *Career Stages of Classroom Teachers* (1989) and *The Kentucky Education Reform: Lessons for America* (1993). She is currently Associate Professor in the Department of Administration and Supervision in the College of Education at the University of Kentucky, Lexington. In 1985 she was selected by *Executive Educator* magazine as one of the "100 national educators to watch." She earned her B.S., M.A.T., and Ed.D. at the University of Pittsburgh.

Jane Clark Lindle, Ph.D., is Associate Professor in the Department of Administration and Supervision at the University of Kentucky. She holds an M.S. in educational administration from the University of Wisconsin—Madison and a B.A. in special education from the University of North Carolina, Chapel Hill. Her previous experience includes serving as a faculty member at the University of Pittsburgh and at Edgewood College of the Sacred Heart in Wisconsin. She has also served as principal for two elementary schools. Her areas of academic interest and expertise include school and community relations, micropolitical aspects of schooling, research methodology, and school policy and governance.

✦ 1 ✦

Creating Constancy of Purpose

TQE's major concern with *constancy of purpose* is a commitment to sustained improvement in student and school performance. This means that a fixed goal or end point is not a sufficient measure of school success; rather, every goal becomes a stepping-stone to the next level of attainment. There is not one point at which any school can simply rest on its reputation, because thinking of improvement as only a move from Point A to Point B obviates the idea of *continuous improvement.*

Many of the characteristics on which schools' reputations are founded are very temporal. For example, more than one high school in the United States defines its success on the basis of the number of its students who win National Merit Scholarships and the number of state and regional sports titles won by its football, cheerleading, basketball, or golf teams. Despite the fact that less than 10% of any school's population can participate in any of these so-called indicators of school success, communities, parents, and school personnel all conspire in the illusion created by these awards and titles. The hollow nature of these markers of school pride and reputation is compounded by the fact that most of those who actually achieve these honors are literally on their way out the door as graduates. Temporal achievements are not only poor indicators of the majority of students' success, they also are not indicative of the broader purposes of schooling.

Precisely because there are broader purposes for schooling, articulating those purposes is not a simple task. In *A Place Called School,*

John Goodlad (1984) enumerates a broad set of goals, commenting, "We want it all." As an aid to school personnel and community, Goodlad suggests four categories of goals: academic goals; vocational goals; social, civic, and cultural goals; and personal goals (pp. 50-56). Among these related goals, clearly both the primary clientele of parents and students and the secondary clientele of the broader community could find general agreement. The specifics, of course, require more negotiation.

This is where Deming's first point is most helpful. A community, including parents, students, secondary clientele, and the school, that is committed to *constancy of purpose for continuous improvement* will have the sustaining dedication necessary to negotiate appropriate goals for its schools. Dedication to constancy of purpose for continuous improvement is a specific commitment by all parties to support education or, in other words, to provide educational capacity. *Educational capacity* consists of the necessary requisites required for optimum learning and achievement. These include student willingness and readiness for learning; parental support and involvement; teacher competence; and school programs, facilities, and supplies; as well as community guarantees to provide adequate supplemental support for any gaps in the capacities of schools, students, or families. This book is about obtaining and sustaining educational capacity, and in this chapter we provide specific suggestions for linking schools and communities to build this capacity.

Any school interested in sustained success must continually enlarge its goals. A fixed five-year plan is not appropriate. With constancy of purpose, a school can never be in the second, third, or fourth year of a five-year plan; it must always be in the first year of an adjusted five-year plan. The trends and experiences identified in the previous year provide the school with the ability to reorient its goals for the next five years. Figure 1.1 illustrates how the principle of constancy of purpose for continuous improvement works for five-year planning cycles. Furthermore, an independent five-year plan is not possible in today's global, technologically advanced political and economic climate. The interdependence of schools and communities is greatly emphasized in a quality environment. Sustained school success requires commitment from a broad range of community groups.

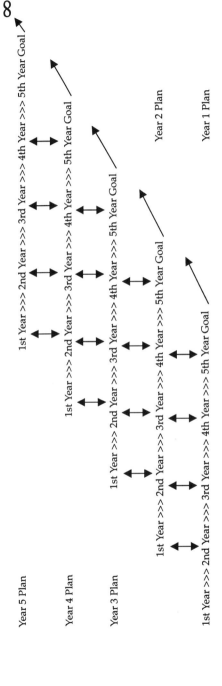

Figure 1.1. Constancy of Purpose for Continuous Improvement in Five-Year Planning
NOTE: ∞ = infinity.

Obviously, schools cannot sustain success without commitment from parents and students. Even with the commitment of parents and students, in today's climate of advanced technology and global economy, schools are ill equipped to supply adequate educational capacity. The establishment of constancy of purpose for schools dictates the necessity of investment from communities, including business and government. In fact, one of the challenges for a school or community interested in quality is how to determine a common purpose, and then how to sustain commitment to achieving that purpose. Why is this so hard for schools, compared with other institutions such as businesses? Schools serve more than one clientele. Schools' primary clientele is made up of students and, depending on the students' maturity, their parents or legal guardians. The secondary clientele is the community, including government and business. The challenge for schools is to serve both clienteles effectively. By their very nature, students and parents will be interested in services that have immediate benefit to them. Communities also will demand services that benefit them. Fortunately, benefits to both groups are often similar; however, there are differences.

Recognizing the similarities and differences in the needs and responses of primary and secondary clienteles is the first step in addressing constancy of purpose. Below, we will identify and explain the services and purposes that schools provide these two clienteles.

Students and Parents
as Primary Clients of Schools

The relationships among particular students, their parents, and the schools form the private side of the public service of education. There is always a tension between the private aspirations, desires, and expectations of parents and students and the public aspirations, desires, and expectations of schools' other clientele: the community. Balancing the private and public purposes of education is a challenge for those who must create constancy of purpose in a school. The initial phase of this balancing act involves a determination of the strength of the private/primary side of the school's relationship with students and parents.

Parents and students often measure their satisfaction with services by their immediate reactions to the activities of the school. A good day or school year will be defined by the students' or parents' perceptions of what was learned and what social activities benefited particular pupils. This is not to suggest that students and parents do not have some long-term expectations about school benefits; for instance, some students and parents will define how "good" a high school is by what kind of postsecondary or work experiences are available to students upon graduation. Primary clients have very individualistic, current senses of school success.

How Good Is Your Client Relationship?

Table 1.1 provides a checklist that a school might use to document the strength of its relationship with its primary clientele. Once school personnel have made efforts to strengthen the school's relations with students and parents, they should solicit the perceptions of those students and parents. Any discrepancies between the efforts the school has documented and the perceptions of students and parents represent weaknesses in the school's relationship with its primary clientele. If such discrepancies between the school and primary clientele are too great, they can have a direct erosive effect on the school's relationship with secondary clientele. In other words, if students and parents are not satisfied with the services and benefits they receive from the school, it will be difficult for the school to obtain the community's interest and commitment.

Dealing With Deficits
Between Efforts and Perceptions

There is no question that changing demographics of the 1980s and early 1990s have had direct effects on schools and their capacity to educate. Despite unwavering expectations of parental support in students' education, teachers and administrators relentlessly report lack of parental involvement in traditional school-family activities.

TABLE 1.1.   Documenting the Primary Client Relationship

What have been the school's efforts to reach out to the primary clientele?

What investments have been made in relationships with students?

Is the school's purpose a unifying guide for all interactions with students and parents?

Are teachers/personnel student oriented or subject oriented?

Are there cocurricular or extracurricular programs to enhance students' success and allegiance to the school?

Does the school empower students to commit to their own learning?

Does the school have a pro-safety/pro-student discipline code?

Has the school provided a legitimate forum for addressing students' concerns?

What investments have been made in parent relationships?

Does the school have a budget and a plan for communication with parents?

Does the school solicit parent involvement and commitment to increasing students' capacity for learning?

Does the school have a welcome/private space for parents to congregate or meet with school personnel?

Has the school provided a legitimate forum for addressing parents' concerns?

What are the students' and parents' perceptions of their relationships with the school?

How much congruence is there between the students' and/or parents' descriptions of the school's purpose and the school's documentation?

How do students and/or parents describe their interactions with school personnel?

Do students and/or parents describe the teachers as student centered or subject oriented?

Do students and/or parents express a responsibility for learning?

Do students and/or parents feel their concerns are addressed?

As educators, we must be aware of the data. If parents do not take part in traditional activities, schools must try some untraditional activities.

TABLE 1.2. Untraditional School-Family Activities

Baby-sitting service	Set up a baby-sitting service using interested older pupils, supervised by an adult. Provide the service during any school-family activities.
Bus the faculty	Put the school faculty on a bus and take them to the students' neighborhoods for a tour. Let students and parents plan the tour route.
Church conferences	Use local churches as neutral territory for school-family activities. Enlist the help of local clergy in reaching out to hard-to-reach students and families.
Friendly circles	Divide parent lists into manageable groups of 10 to 12 people and set up regular meetings for these circles. Let the circles operate with and without the presence of school personnel.
Movie night	Rent a movie and invite the families. Let them bring snacks. (Do not charge admission for this. Besides limiting potential participation for this family night, you could get into legal trouble for trying to make money from the use of commercial movies.)
Roller-skating	Create a wholesome activity that can involve families of teachers and students. Informal conversations among the adults can go a long way toward developing the necessary support system for more formal educational activities.
Talent search	Discover "hidden" talents of students and their parents. Call them for their expertise in their areas before picking up the phone book for less personal and more expensive responses to school needs.

We list some suggestions in Table 1.2. Once such untraditional methods have helped to establish informal relationships with families, more traditional and formal activities can be introduced. The dominant barrier to good relations between families and schools is a mismatch between the informal, personalized world of family life

and the formal, conservative atmosphere of school institutions
(Lindle, 1989; Lindle & Boyd, 1991; Litwak & Meyer, 1974).

How Relationships With Primary Clientele Affect Secondary Clientele

The shift in demographics over the past couple of decades has
implications for relationships between schools and their secondary
clientele. A few decades ago, parents were a large, dominant proportion of the secondary clientele of schools. Most businesspeople were
parents; most government officials, agents, and workers were parents;
most taxpaying members of the community were parents. Today, in
some communities, school parents are not in the majority. In some
places, owing to increases in single-person households and other
demographic shifts, as many as 85% of community members do
not have children in school. Such statistics have powerful implications for linkages between schools and their primary and secondary
clienteles.

Communities have a different sort of attention span than that of
the primary clientele. They are not as attentive to the daily routines
of schools as are primary clientele; rather, they focus on critical events.
For example, communities will pay attention to any aberrant events,
such as reports of weapons or violence at schools. The business
segment of the community will attend to marked changes in the skills
or abilities of new employees and ascribe deficits to the schools.
Secondary clients react spontaneously to unusual critical events or
long-term trends.

Because the natural links between parents and communities have
eroded, schools need to pay more attention to bridging these gaps.
If taxpayers feel that schools are taking a large chunk of their income
and they are receiving no direct benefits, then they will be even less
tolerant of schools where parents and students are disaffected.
Schools must tend to the needs and perceptions of their primary
clientele because those needs and perceptions will have a strong
influence on the needs and perceptions of the secondary clientele.
Both groups require careful documentation and monitoring efforts.

Business, Government, and Community as Secondary Clients

Another factor influencing the relationship between schools and business, government, and community are the resources that schools provide to the other sectors of the community. What are those resources? A potential workforce, a potential tax base from potential property owners and income producers—in other words, productive citizens are the long-term returns from education. The primary clients of schools are the resources for the secondary clients.

What Is the Assessment of These Relationships?

Assessment of schools' relationships with business, government, and community includes documentation, monitoring, and surveys. Responsible assessment includes matching investments from these clients with outcomes. Table 1.3 lists a variety of investments that various segments of the secondary clientele typically make in schools. Although the actual dollar figures represented by the traditional investments of secondary clients in schools are not insignificant, the list looks rather paltry because the investments are limited to non-labor-intensive resources. There are some repercussions for schools because of the nature of the items in this list. Because the dollar investment is significant in the short term, secondary clients have high expectations for tangible evidence of short-term school success. Because the labor investment is trivial, secondary clients are naturally ignorant of the long-term, and sometimes intangible, evidence of school success.

Identifying Needs for Further Investment

One way to strengthen schools' connections to secondary clientele is to increase secondary clients' level of commitment, that is, expand the level of investment. Each segment of the secondary clientele requires an analysis of the benefits it could derive from increased investment in schools. "We need to get beyond the immediate PR payoff of a businessperson handing a big check to a school official. We need to get into deeper levels of involvement of

TABLE 1.3. Secondary Clientele's Current Investments in Schools

Business investments
    Provide a corporate tax base for school funding
    Make special donations of equipment or money for school programs
    Provide product samples for student and classroom use

Government investments
    Provide property tax and, in some cases, local income tax revenues
    for school budget
    Make the local transit system available for school transportation
    needs

Community investments   Vary depending on locale

businesses and schools," says Carolyn W. Snyder, coordinator of the Partnership for Kentucky School Reform in Lexington (personal communication, June 25, 1993). Communities that have orchestrated new means of involving schools and business, government, and the general community have adopted a more long-term view of the nature of school-community relationships. These communities report that both schools and business must reorient their thinking more strategically to ways in which their collaboration can produce benefits to the community.

Project Parent is an intercommunity project established through the Mayor's Office in Owensboro, Kentucky. Mayor David Adkisson, with the endorsement of a variety of community agencies and businesses, has targeted support for parents as a prime goal for the community of Owensboro, the third-largest city in Kentucky. This may seem to be an atypical agenda for a mayor, but Project Parent represents an attempt to do something about dismal demographic statistics on teen pregnancy, infant mortality, and other troubling trends witnessed by all segments of the community, from law enforcement to schools (Crossley, 1993). Mayor Adkisson and Project Parent Director Vikki LeClair Mills visit various civic, business, and community organizations to introduce the concept. They include in their introduction "shopping lists" targeted to specific community sectors. A few of their shopping list items are displayed in Table 1.4.

TABLE 1.4. Shopping Lists for Further Investments

For businesses and corporations

Form an employee parent-management task force to evaluate possible company policies on the following:

Flextime for parent-school activities

Sick leave for parents of children who are ill

Extended leave for family crises

Offer lunch forums for employees who are parenting (remember that many grandparents are rearing grandchildren).

Support groups could be developed.

Short presentations and discussions that deal with parenting could be offered.

Use the internal company newsletter to share information about parenting.

For churches

Advertise in the church newsletter the community services available to parents and families.

Add books and videos about parenting to the church library or set up an interlibrary loan with the nearest school library.

Sponsor a forum for parents on the local schools. Get school system personnel to be involved in the presentation.

For community organizations

Do family activities rather than activities for members only.

Use parenting as a yearlong focus for your regular programs.

Coordinate volunteer transportation for students/parents who need it for appointments, after-school activities, lessons, and so on.

SOURCE: Project Parent. Used by permission of the Office of the Mayor of Owensboro, Kentucky, and Project Parent.

Innovative ideas such as these are generated by identifying the kinds of resources to which the particular segment of the community is uniquely suited. By offering a long list of possibilities, schools, businesses, community groups, and government can move beyond traditional and transitory monetary investments to more sustaining commitments. These commitments can be strategically oriented toward maintaining the constancy of purpose necessary for school/student success.

Accountability and Assurances

Changing the investments of business, community, and government will necessitate a change in the expected reporting mechanisms. For instance, businesses that pour money into a school naturally expect outcomes that can be reported in the school's budgetary process. This expectation is linked to the way that businesses commonly track monetary revenues and expenditures. Change a business's investment from financial to labor-intensive projects with parents or students, and the expected means of reporting changes. Bottom-line reports are no longer sufficient. Furthermore, a business that is truly involved in the lives of a school's primary clients has constant sources of feedback and monitoring, through its employees who provide the project's labor.

Issues of accountability and assurance are potentially volatile when trust is low. There is nothing about a financial investment that inherently builds trust. Labor-intensive projects, on the other hand, are grounded in building personal relationships. The very nature of personal relationships intensifies opportunities for building trust, and bonds of trust are fundamental for communicating school success to either primary or secondary clientele of schools.

Communicating School/Student Success

The old boundaries of what constitutes a school system are changing—broadening and expanding. Traditionally, they have included the geographic limits of the enrollment boundaries of the district, the physical plant of each school, and the staff employed by the school system. In some more enlightened districts, parents and children have been considered an integral part of the school system. Today, these boundaries are expanding to serve a different type of system. This new school system incorporates many other systems, such as the juvenile justice system, the health care system, the social services system, local systems of government, communities, local service organizations, and chambers of commerce. Such change was predicted in various ways in the 1970s by researchers such as

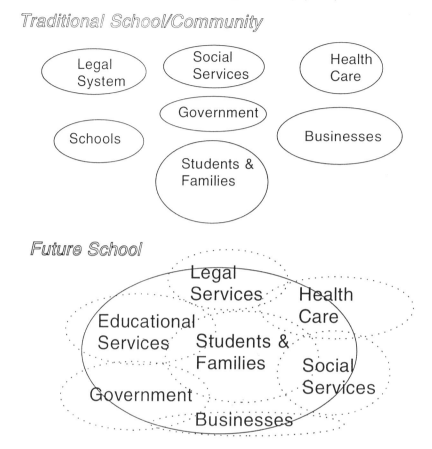

Figure 1.2. Transforming School Systems

Bronfenbrenner (1974) and Hobbes (1978); we call this highly integrated system *Future School* (see Figure 1.2).

One of the greatest problems in building this newly integrated community school system is in defining the unity of purpose for which it operates. Deming (1993) describes a system as "a network of interdependent components that work together to try to accomplish the aim of the system" (p. 50). No system can exist without an aim. To date, the aim of the newly integrated school system is emerging. It is not clear to everyone who works in the system just what it is trying to accomplish. At present, far too many participants in the emerging integrated school system that we call Future School give their allegiance to the subparts of the system and not to the integrated whole. This leads to competition among the subgroups, creates fear, and fails to enable the integrated system to develop a constancy of purpose. Before the aim of Future School can be defined, a feeling of trust must be developed among the subgroups.

The school leader who would like to build Future School should begin by establishing positive relationships with the leaders of the subgroups who will become part of the integrated system. The process begins with the creation of a core planning committee. Membership of this committee can vary from district to district, depending on a number of variables, including the following:

- The size of the system
- The population density of the service area (urban, suburban, or rural)
- The nature and type of social service entities in the service area
- The socioeconomic status of the service area
- The political liaisons and history of the school governance bodies, school board, central administration, and civic governance bodies, mayor's or executive director's office, city or county government, and judicial and law enforcement leadership
- The history of interagency cooperation or civic collaboration in the community

As with many new ventures, it is best to start in a small way. Because the current focus in school restructuring is the individual school, the steps suggested here could be carried out by the building principal. If the school system is countywide or city based, these steps could serve as a guide for an initiative to be carried out by the superintendent of schools. In some of the real-world examples we use in this book, the initiative for generating closer school-community/business/government links was assumed by third parties acting as liaisons between schools and targeted sectors of the community. There is no one position that might be best suited to developing these connections, but it is critical that they be forged.

Traditional Communications
and Definitions of School Success

Within the traditional relationships between schools and both their primary and secondary clienteles, very little daily interaction takes place. Most communications are periodic. Parents and students can expect report cards four to six times a year. The broader community may learn nothing about schools beyond an annual meeting on the budget reported tersely in the local media.

In the past decade, the broader community's information about schools was amplified to "wall charting" of achievement test scores. The unit of analysis depended on the level of government promulgating the wall chart. National officials offered wall charts of state-level achievement data. State-level offices provided district-level information. The district could be broken down into a wall chart of individual school performance. Other than a ranking of schools, school districts, or states, the achievement data provided very little information about schools or even students' success. Worse, some communities were faced with information suggesting that they were the worst in the nation, state, region, county, or district. Yet these same communities could point with pride to alternate indicators of success, such as the percentage of students who graduate and go on to postsecondary education. These wall-charting experiences probably illustrated more about the need to establish constancy of purpose than about the relative worth of any particular school or district.

Identifying Community Indicators of Success

The integrated nature of Future School demands more complex levels of accounting for school/student success. Each subpart of the system has a traditional set of records tied to specific subpart goals or aims. In the transformed, integrated Future School, these individual records, goals, or aims must be reconciled to the overriding purpose of school/student success.

Here is a specific example. In many communities, school absenteeism is correlated to juvenile arrests. Schools keep records on absences. Juvenile justice systems keep records on complaints and arrests.

The juvenile justice system and the schools, as part of Future School, will be able not only to monitor overall absentee/complaint or arrest rates but to get involved with monitoring individual absenteeism and complaints/arrests. With an integrated accounting system, the focus on school/student success can shift from a general reading of demographic trends to specific information on individual performance. This specific information can be used to address individual needs and to plan for individual improvement.

Reconciling Community Indicators With Global Indicators

Communities sometimes are lulled into complacency about their schools because they may not be using globally accepted indicators of school/student success. Some communities find schools to be the focus of social life because of an outstanding sports program, for instance, but are not informed about the draining of resources from the academic program. It takes a wall chart, or other aberrant or critical event, to arouse the community's interest in parts of the school that are not as well-known as its social aspects.

In establishing constancy of purpose for Future School, all the integrated subparts must be informed of the global indicators that affect definitions of school success. In fact, data that go beyond the familiar subsystem reports must be included in the new information system of Future School (see Chapter 2 for more on information systems). Technological innovations make global indicators of school/student success more accessible. Benchmark data for schools/students, regionally, nationally, and globally, are available and can be helpful in the establishment of strategic goals for maintaining constancy of purpose in schools (see Chapter 4 for more on benchmarks).

In Future School, the subsystem in which professional educational leadership is dominant must access, collect, and maintain benchmark educational data. Data on this vast scope appropriate to the other subsets should be maintained by the professionals in those areas. Law enforcement officers should monitor local, national, and global indicators of illegal activity. Social service agencies should track data relevant to social indicators locally, nationally, and globally. Each subpart remains specialized in terms of its expertise in recording, analyzing, and interpreting trends, but all subparts become more collaborative in planning and implementing strategies for addressing these trends.

Supplying Opportunities for Community Monitoring

The accessibility of information accounting for school/student success must be communicated across the community. Sometimes the best way to inform the community about school/student success is to provide opportunities for direct monitoring. Traditionally, school performances, fairs, and sporting events are staged means of communicating, in an episodic manner, the ways that schools/students are successful. However, as is true of investments in education, monitoring cannot be accomplished in a non-labor-intensive fashion. Labor-intensive involvement in the activities of Future School will include hands-on opportunities for monitoring by the community.

Key Terms and Concepts

Benchmarks. Indicators of educational progress with linkage to local, national, or international standards.

Constancy of purpose. The idea that until there is stability around intention no system can begin to initiate meaningful change.

Demographics. Key community or school descriptors of population size, economic conditions, and educational attainment.

Educational capacity. The support system for basic needs, nurturing, and good health, which constitute the foundation of readiness for school.

Future School. Our name for the concept of an integrated school-community investment in increased educational capacity and school/student success.

Primary school clients. Students and parents who are directly affected by schools.

Relationship assessment. Activities that include documentation, monitoring, and surveying to find out perceptions of schools' relationships with students, parents, business, government, and the community.

Secondary school clients. Business, government, and communities— indirect clients of schools.

System. A collection of parts that, when working together, are able to attain an objective that none could reach individually.

Untraditional school-family activities. Informal services that are not currently an ordinary part of those most often considered in school-family relationships.

References

Bronfenbrenner, U. (1974). The origins of alienation. *Scientific American, 231*(2), 53-61.

Crossley, C. (1993, March 1). Owensboro is putting priority on its families. *Courier-Journal* (Louisville, KY), pp. 1, 5.

Deming, W. E. (1993). *The new economics for industry, government, education.* Cambridge, MA: MIT Center for Advanced Engineering Study.

Goodlad, J. I. (1984). *A place called school.* New York: McGraw-Hill.

Hobbes, N. (1978). Families, schools, and communities: An ecosystem for children. *Teachers College Record, 79*, 767-787.

Lindle, J. C. (1989). What do parents want from principals and teachers? *Educational Leadership, 47*(2), 12-14.

Lindle, J. C., & Boyd, W. L. (1991). Parents, professionalism, and partnership in school-community relations. *International Journal of Educational Research, 15*, 323-337.

Litwak, E., & Meyer, H. J. (1974). *School, family and neighborhood: The theory and practice of school-community relations.* New York: Columbia University Press.

✧ **2** ✧

Leadership for Change:
From Competition to Cooperation

An integrated network for school support requires cooperation, not competition. Successful leadership is not the hubris of one-upmanship, but nurturing that forges strong linkages among partners who understand and trust one another.

Cooperation and collaborative leadership can provide more powerful relief for various social issues faced by schools than Herculean assaults through legislation, regulation, or even by individual school personnel, parents, or community members. Within schools' primary clientele, school personnel nurture leadership among parents and students as well as among each other. Among schools' secondary clientele, schools respond to and promote leaders from the community, government, and business who can address issues that improve school/student success.

Benefits of Cooperation

It is almost axiomatic in these days of scarce resources to note that shared resources create outcomes greater than the sum of the parts. Educational outcomes are no different. Students with interested, committed parents do well in school. Students with good teachers do well in school. Students with both good teachers and interested, committed parents show gains beyond expectations (Comer, 1980;

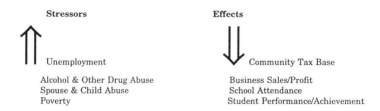

Figure 2.1. Socioeconomic Stressors and Community and Student/School Effects

Epstein, 1987). As the socioeconomic issues facing students and schools increase, the crucial support system of parents and teachers also is affected. Few other adults in the community feel compelled to shore up support for children who are not their own. James Coleman (1987, 1991) refers to the network supporting children as "social capital" and notes that such capital has substantially eroded. Under these conditions, capacity for education is threatened. The links among community, business, and government become pivotal.

Assessing Local Community Benefits

Community benefits from collaborative leadership efforts are directly linked to the abundance or scarcity of local resources as well as the severity of local socioeconomic issues. Some of the socioeconomic stresses that affect communities and thus student well-being are also detrimental to school/student success. These stressors and their effects are illustrated in Figure 2.1. Dealing with student achievement in isolation from other community issues is like picking lint off of one side of a sweater that is unraveling from the other side. The side being picked at might look better, but the whole sweater won't last for long!

Business and community leaders know that good schools are an important part of attracting new business and thus new jobs. School leaders have good reason to expect cooperation when they seek community, business, and government involvement. Among the benefits found by schools that reach out are willing responses from local businesses and government. Most business and community leaders are frustrated that schools typically do not reach out to them or accept their offers of help. School leaders frequently complain that what businesses and government offer is not really useful. All parties must realize that aid should not consist only of businesses donating to schools their castoff materials or funding short-term projects; rather, true aid includes careful planning and interaction of schools, business, and government on what is useful for the entire community and its schools and what is necessary to address community and school needs. In other words, schools and their communities must assess their social capital.

One current approach to addressing social capital through increasing educational capacity is the linking of schools and social agencies. In Kentucky, Family Resource/Youth Services Centers (FRYSCs) have been competitively funded by the state legislature. Among other requirements for obtaining funding, schools and communities seeking the establishment of an FRYSC must document need. Successful grants are obtained by those schools and communities that have used broad-based community data sources. Table 2.1 shows the variety of data sources used by one of Kentucky's new FRYSCs. Data-based decision making and needs assessments will be discussed further in the remainder of this chapter and in Chapter 4.

Interagency Planning

The heart of a collaborative relationship is trust (we deal specifically with issues of building trust in Chapter 3). In Deming's language, trust is also the act of "driving out fear." Barriers to subgroup interactions and total commitment to pride in workmanship must be achieved simultaneously if we are to promote high-quality communities and education.

Interagency planning is impossible if there is fear of inspection, protection of turf, or pride only in self-aggrandizement. Planning requires access to a variety of data that are indicators of total community success. Indicators taken from specific community sectors in isolation are not sufficient for planning. Some of the broad-based community data that are useful are shown in Table 2.1. Here we will describe the means by which pride can be a collective rather

TABLE 2.1. Data Sources for Assessing Social Capital

School data sources, disaggregated by socioeconomic status, race, ethnicity, and gender
Grade-level retention rates
Failure rates
Absentee rates
Dropout rates
Discipline referrals
  Suspension rates
  Expulsion rates
Proportions of student body assigned to remedial or special education
Proportions of graduates who are employed, enrolled in post-secondary education, or in the military
Proportions of the student body eligible for free lunches

Community-level data sources
Census data
  Population size and density
  Household configurations
Chamber of commerce data
  Extent and type of businesses/economic base
  Projected business growth and development plans
  Availability of day care
  Recreation resources
Extension agency data
  Types and utilization level of services
  Conditions and projections of agribusiness economic base
Health care data
  Types, access to, and availability of medical services
  Summary data on incidence of service utilization
  Incidence of teen pregnancy
  Rate of infant mortality
  Treatment rate for alcohol and other drug abuse
Municipality/local civic/government data
  Types, access to, and availability of municipal services
  Projected community growth and development plans
  Transportation issues
  Law enforcement data
    Crime rate

Juvenile offenses rate
Domestic violence and abuse incidence
Social services data
Type, access, and availability of services
Unemployment rate
Level of welfare support

---

than personal experience, and how barriers between the subsystems of Future School can be removed.

Ownership and Pride

Deming's point concerning reinstituting pride and joy in workmanship can be relevant to interagency planning. A key feature about pride is that it breeds further commitment, which is an issue in building the concept of Future School.

The subsystems of Future School—education, social and legal services, and other businesses or government agencies—have well-established traditions of operating independently and often competitively. A strong link to the activities of schooling will require some built-in opportunities and policies promoting links to communities.

Project Parent in Owensboro, Kentucky, and the Kentucky Partnership for School Reform both encourage businesses to adopt policies that promote involvement in local schools. Both suggest that businesses adopt personnel policies that do not penalize parents for taking leave for an offspring's school activities or illness. Another personnel policy promoted by both organizations is one that encourages employees without children in school to participate as tutors, mentors, or aides in schools.

Carolyn Snyder of the Kentucky Partnership for School Reform reports that opportunities for employees to be involved in schools must be negotiated around the business's structure and the individual school's or teachers' needs. She says that in these negotiations, ideas are framed as "what will make a difference for kids." Snyder tells the following story of what happened when a bank and some elementary teachers asked each other what they could do jointly to make a difference for kids.

The teachers were trying to implement more hands-on mathematics. The bank employees really did not know how they could help, but teachers and bank employees planning together came up with this solution. Teachers were struggling to make enough materials for their math program and still keep up with students. The bank set aside a space in the employees' break room where employees could spend some of their break time cutting and pasting math materials for the busy teachers. In this way, the teachers had more time to devote to instructional activities, and bank employees felt useful in providing resources. The bank employees were also more informed about the kinds of math instruction taking place in the schools. The teachers felt some pride in sharing this information, and the bank employees felt some ownership in student learning and success (C. Snyder, personal communication, June 25, 1993).

Removing Barriers

The ideal of total quality is advanced when subgroups work holistically in a system. Finding the catalyst to stimulate separate parts to act in concert is not easy. Although building trust is certainly a factor, remnants of the old internal rewards and sanctions must also be dealt with.

What keeps a teacher from working in coordination with parents, and vice versa? What prevents a social service agency from keeping teachers informed of student needs? What are the official and informal barriers that prevent even our most optimistic readers from fully believing that Future School is possible?

Most of the answers to these questions lie in maintaining the status quo. Future School is not possible without a complete disruption of what everyone does now, and such radical change cannot be achieved in incremental stages. And at the same time that giant upheavals require patience, they are quite painful. By asking and answering questions concerning what prevents all segments of the community from tackling problems together, we begin to identify the barriers. In Chapter 3, we will provide specific steps for addressing the barriers to collaboration among subsystems and subgroups. Without removing those barriers, decision making and goal setting become futile exercises, for no subsystem or subgroup can have sufficient data to make good decisions.

Making Decisions

Today, standard operating procedure for schools, businesses, government, and communities is to make long- and short-range plans. The very nature of planning requires analysis of current trends and future projections of data about education, economics, and political systems. Strategic planning requires making decisions that have long-term effects on the nature and collection of further data to monitor trends and projections. Data collection and management have important functions in the decision-making process for each of these groups. The problem is, each group makes decisions that have potential for affecting not only its own future but the future of the other groups. As long as the decision-making process and data collection and analysis are isolated to each group, none of the groups ever have adequate information on which to make good decisions.

Developing Information Systems
for Decision Making

An information system consists of the routine acquisition of data, trends, and projections necessary for planning and decision making. Although the effective use of information technology is a critical strategic resource for any organization, integrative information systems are becoming even more potent and vital strategic resources for communities (Emery, 1987).

The key elements of an information system for Future School are listed in Table 2.2. These elements become the basis for cooperation, as described in Chapter 3. In order to have access to these elements, the various subgroups using the system must negotiate issues of confidentiality and security. Keep in mind that confidentiality and security are volatile issues in competitive systems; in collaborative systems, these issues are not as important. If access to data or information is a hot topic in a community, this is evidence that the barriers to collaboration have not been eliminated.

TABLE 2.2. Requirements for Collaborative Data Systems

Hardware
  Compatibility
  Convertibility
  Flexibility for updates and expansion
  Functional task capabilities for storage, analysis, and
    communications
  Reasonable, accessible costs for all users
  Centralized maintenance service and planning
Software
  Compatibility
  Convertibility
  Flexibility for adapting to specific application adaptations
  Interactive, real-world language, environment, and applications
  Functional task capabilities for data entry, storage, analysis, presen-
    tation, and communications
  Reasonable, accessible costs for all users
  Centralized training and support for user development
  Centralized programming and adaptation of application services
  Centralized archiving, updates, and planning
Information management
  Centralized planning for data identification and collection
    procedures
  Centralized scheduling of data renewal and updates of analyses
  Centralized management of routine schedules for archiving,
    analysis, reports, and presentations
  Centralized monitoring of data storage, retrieval, usage, and com-
    munications tasks
  Centralized monitoring and updates of software and hardware
    environments

To some who are new to Deming's philosophy, his Point 11, *eliminate numerical quotas,* seems somewhat contradictory to the information system we are recommending here. In fact, Deming is supportive of data-based decision making. Statistical analysis of the issues faced by an organization is one of Deming's approaches. On the other hand, Deming promotes the elimination of numerical quotas because the decisions to pursue particular quotas are often made arbitrarily. Such outcome measures are somewhat suspect in their association to current conditions or future conditions. For example, if quotas are based on current conditions, changing and future conditions are not taken into account. As most statisticians know, changing and future conditions cut down on the reliability of projections. Even with sophisticated statistical techniques, there is always a margin of error. With TQE, quality is not possible if it is excused by a margin of error.

In an analysis of what this particular point means to education, Blankenstein (1992, pp. 73-74) makes the following assertions on the limitations of quotas:

- The goals are usually arbitrarily set.
- Setting quotas leads to marginal performance.
- Appraisal of individual performance is unfair and misguided.
- Merit pay destroys teamwork.
- Individual appraisal nourishes fear.
- A system of individual appraisal increases variability in the desired performance.

Throughout this book we will introduce a number of data-collection, analysis, and decision-making techniques. None of these presentations are intended to imply that we recommend the establishment of quota systems.

Dealing With Scarce Resources

As we continually reiterate throughout this book, neither schools nor families have sufficient resources to maintain the education capacity or social capital that today's and tomorrow's children require. Advances in technology as well as global political and economic forces compel us to plan an education for children that introduces them to broad, complex academic, social, and vocational issues much earlier in their schooling than was the case in the past. The current structure of schools tends to isolate children from the broader, more complex communities in which they and their families exist. Families

TABLE 2.3. Resources and Sources: Expanding Social Capital and Educational Capacity

Resources	Sources
Financial and volunteer support for a child-care unit	Civic club
Child/parent safety information	Union local
Immunization clinic	Restaurant
School/parent recognition dinner	Florist, appliance business
Lunchtime seminars for parents	Bank
Interactive displays for parents and children	Museum
Family night discounts once a week	Golf business
Advertising for parent-child activities	Church
Task force on sick time and flextime for school projects	Physicians' clinic
Books and materials for family support	Public library
Special discounts for sporting events	College

might be able to provide personal support for these more complex environments, but they are ill equipped to develop the academic, social, and vocational capacities necessary for survival. Schools cannot remain isolated; they must serve these needs. Thus, as communities become more complex, the resources required for increasing social capital and educational capacity must be drawn from a number of sources. This pooling of resources is far more likely to handle complicated environments than isolated attempts by schools or families.

In Owensboro, Kentucky, the Mayor's Office, through Project Parent, has taken advantage of the resources of businesses and community organizations and agencies to increase the educational capacity of schools and parents. Table 2.3 lists a few of the contributions that have been made and the types of groups, agencies, and businesses making the contributions.

Celebration: Leveraging Even *More* Benefits

Deming's point about restoring pride and joy is essentially a reminder of why people are likely to be generous with their time and energy. Pride and joy are happy manifestations of good work. If people are happy, then they are likely to do more of whatever brought them that happiness. The Mayor's Office in Owensboro knows this and has events planned all through the year for the celebration of both families and the groups contributing resources to bolster family life. These acts of celebration are not mere public relations events but a means of strengthening commitment to the project. Through celebration, there exists a public record of commitment and success. With public witness of the success thus far, these groups then redouble their efforts to find more resources for the project. Celebrations frequently are the means to more collaboration.

Schools as Centers
for Community Growth

The traditional, limited view of professional development is that teachers must continually learn in order to teach. This view is limiting because it keeps the spotlight only on teachers in classrooms. There are teachers all over the community. True, many are not professional teachers, but they possess special and specialized knowledge from which professional teachers and their students— and even parents and other community members—can benefit. The new professional development concept is that the whole community must be engaged in professional development, by creating learning communities, intellectual partnerships, and opportunities for mutual mentoring.

Learning Communities

Learning communities are groups of citizens, students, parents, and teachers who come together to form partnerships in learning. Such partnerships may involve special projects, such as a community garden, or they may involve meeting some pressing community need, such as increasing the number of crossing guards for unsafe roads leading to schools.

Intellectual Partnerships and Mutual Mentoring

Intellectual partnerships and mutual mentoring are largely adult-to-adult relationships in which adult learners pursue topics of mutual interest. A classical music club that meets to discuss great symphonies and then attend live concerts is an example. Various adults in the community may have special interests, such as stamp or baseball card collecting, that may prove fascinating to adults and children alike.

Community Knowledge Resources

The most obvious way to identify the resources in the school community is to survey community members. The primary community for schools is parents—parents who have jobs in community business and government, parents who own their own businesses, and parents who may have specialized talents or occupations to share with the school. Oddly enough, in the mistaken belief that asking parents their occupations violates some confidentiality laws, many schools do not have even card-file records of parents' occupations, talents, or expertise. This information is easily obtained when students register or enroll in the school.

Surveying the Community

A survey of the talent and expertise in the rest of the community is as easy as opening the phone book. With only a little more time, it is possible to unearth hidden talents in the school community by using a survey. An example of such a survey appears here as Exhibit 2.1. Using this survey, a school can develop its own directory of community expertise and find ways to use the talents discovered in the community. Table 2.4 shows some ways in which a directory of community expertise can be put to use.

Community Survey of
Professional Development Resources*

_____ School [or School District] is searching for hidden talents and expertise. Will you help us with our investigation? It will take you only about 10 minutes to answer the following questions and return your responses in the enclosed, self-addressed, stamped envelope.

___ What do you consider your field of expertise?

___ Are there ways in which schools could better educate children about this field?

___ What would you do to further this field with students?

___ Are you willing to help with a group of students in this field?

Check off the types of activities you feel comfortable doing with school students:

___ Touring facilities where you work

___ Demonstrating your work on the job or in a classroom

___ Speaking to parents and students in a career-day workshop

___ Scheduling one-to-one meetings with parents and students about your work

___ Speaking to a classroom of students

___ Visiting classrooms with some of your coworkers to talk about your field

Is there someone else we should contact about working with students in your field? Please give us their name(s), address(es), and phone number(s). Let us know if we should (or should not) use your name when contacting them.

Thanks for your help!

*Adapt this survey to fit the language and values of your community. Attention to local language and values can increase your survey response rate.

Exhibit 2.1.

TABLE 2.4. Ways to Use the Directory of Community Expertise

Business and industry trends
    For teachers, students, parents, and interested community
    To learn side by side
    To broaden skills and repertoires
    To implement curriculum updates
    To Increase mutual commitment to community excellence
Career awareness
    For teachers, students, parents, and local job seekers
    To broaden opportunity
    To increase commitment to educational prerequisites
Outstanding lecture series
    For teachers, students, parents, senior citizens, and other interested community members
    To enhance community activities
    To broaden community involvement

Schools often have limited information on the cultural diversity of their communities. Unless race is an indicator of local culture, many cultures that are not tied to race remain hidden. Another survey, such as that used to gain information about community expertise, can be used to identify community cultural diversity and to develop a directory of cultures as a resource for the school's development of global and international awareness. The school can also plan to celebrate that diversity with activities such as the one described below.

International School/Community Theme

At least once a year, the school and community could collaborate on a monthlong international theme. This theme would be the basis for study at all levels in the school system and for activities within the community. For example, if the community has a significant population with cultural links to the Pacific Rim, the theme for the integrated school-community unit could be "20th-Century Life in the Pacific Rim." At every school, within every classroom, the context of instruction could highlight Asia, especially the Pacific Rim, and its influences on both the 20th and 21st centuries. Each school in the district could choose to focus on a different aspect or country. Within the community, the local library could sponsor a travel series about the countries. Citizens with cultural links to the Pacific Rim could be invited to speak in the schools. Cable television and satellite dish businesses could provide school and community links to programming and media relevant to the Pacific Rim. Study groups could be organized to focus on current issues related to U.S. and local relations with the countries of the area. The local bank could provide displays of the currency used in the various nations as well as offer students and adults an opportunity to learn about exchange rates. Local grocery stores could feature food from Pacific Rim countries. The local newspaper could print recipes, human interest stories, and news from the nations of study. The post office could exhibit related stamps. Merchants could decorate their windows around the theme. The local community center could offer concerts and art exhibits relevant to the study. Local theater groups could feature drama or other shows from the region. Local television news programs could feature news and weather from the area of study. Reenactments of major historical events could be organized that could include community members of all ages.

Through this integrated study, learning would be taking place throughout the community. Because everyone would be aware of the theme, it could be the basis for family discussions at the dinner table and other exchanges of ideas and opinions, as well as a catalyst for total community growth. This type of activity reinforces the interconnected nature of schools, businesses, and government. Of course, the month of study would culminate in a community celebration highlighting people in the community with these cultural links.

The whole point in moving from competition to cooperation is to create a larger synergistic educational environment. This capitalizes on educational capacity for both children and adults. Educational capacity is increased by tapping into the social capital of the richer educational environment of the community. School-focused staff development must give way to community development, in which the school is simply one center among many that engage in personal and professional development for purposes of enriching the school's curriculum and programs. By forming linkages with individuals, groups, and agencies, the school is—and especially its students are—embraced in a web of interrelationships that are collaborative and cooperative.

Key Terms and Concepts

Collaboration. Purposeful activity by individuals or groups to further both individual and collective goals and ends.

Community-level data sources. Information available locally that can be used to describe a given set of activities, issues, or problems in a community.

Cooperation. Activity undertaken in which the goals of two or more individuals, groups, or agencies are compatible and pursued simultaneously.

Educational futures. An anticipated state of schooling with effective partnership and collaboration among a broad variety of agencies that exist but that are not necessarily working *with* schools in pursuit of a common agenda.

Information system. A network of data that facilitates planning, goal development, and effective decision making.

Leadership. Actions taken by individuals that influence, guide, nurture, and direct other individuals or groups to pursue a given topic or take an action.

Social capital. The idea that education depends on a support system of adults both in and outside of schools to provide resources and to increase educational capacity.

References

Blankenstein, A. M. (1992). Lessons from enlightened corporations. *Educational Leadership, 49*(6), 71-75.

Coleman, J. S. (1987). Families and schools. *Educational Researcher, 16*(6), 32-38.

Coleman, J. S. (1991). What constitutes educational opportunity? *Oxford Review of Education, 17,* 155-159.

Comer, J. P. (1980). *School power.* New York: Free Press.

Emery, J. C. (1987). *Management information systems: The critical strategic resource.* New York: Oxford University Press.

Epstein, J. L. (1987). Parent involvement: What research says to administrators. *Education and Urban Society, 19,* 119-136.

✧ **3** ✧

Building Trust Among the Partners

Trust is the glue that holds together any coalition built among schools, business, government, and the community. From Deming's 14 points, the following are particularly salient regarding trust:

- Create constancy of purpose.
- Institute leadership.
- Drive out fear.
- Break down barriers between staff.

We have already reviewed creating constancy of purpose and we will continue to point out the requirements for leadership. In Chapter 2, we provided considerable focus for Deming's seventh point, *institute leadership.* Under TQE, leadership becomes a community requisite for implementing the coalitions that build educational capacity. The leadership described by Deming suggests a collaborative, imaginative approach to participation in planning and decision making.

Deming's Point 8, *drive out fear,* is salient to this chapter because no collaborative effort is possible unless the anxieties of the participants are settled. Furthermore, the factory/inspection model of the past has been focused primarily on catching wrongdoers and eliminating them. Creativity and imagination have been squelched under this approach, because deviating from the norm has meant the same thing as "doing wrong." This is a critical point for our argument in this volume. Schools must ensure that their primary clients are treated with respect rather than accusations and abuse. Moreover, schools must learn to accept the concerns of students and parents without becoming defensive. With secondary clients, schools that wish to drive out fear must drop competitive approaches with government, businesses, and community. Instead, schools must take a more cooperative approach to addressing community and primary clientele issues.

Fear is also at the root of barriers separating different staff areas. Schools should interpret Deming's Point 9, *break down barriers between staff*, in its most complex form. Schools must break down the barriers within their own internal structures, between schools and primary clientele, and between schools and their communities. School staff must be encouraged to drop territorial and status-enhancing behavior. Instead, the focus must be on sharing expertise and resources in addressing the needs of primary and secondary clientele. School staff should be prepared to facilitate student communication with parents. School personnel should reach out to the pockets of expertise in the community that can be leveraged to expand and to refine the educational process.

Driving out fear and breaking down barriers are accomplished by (a) engaging in team building and (b) eliminating those practices and traditions that create fear within and outside of schools. Most of those things are encouraged by competitive situations requiring that there be "winners and losers."

Selecting the Team

Every community has a number of citizens who are considered movers and shakers. These leaders come from every facet of the community: lay citizens, business leaders, government officials, agency administrators, and parents. Many of these leaders already understand the interconnected nature of the various elements that make up the community and recognize that the community's future well-being is dependent on the ability of all elements to grow and prosper. These individuals understand the need for a community aim and constancy of purpose. However, the development of a unified system that incorporates many other independent systems is a task of gargantuan magnitude:

> Just as a lasting and comprehensive service system for children cannot be established without the participation of the school, neither can schools meet children's comprehensive needs without the participation of other agencies. School leaders have increasingly realized that the education system alone has neither the ability nor political clout to address the full range of children's problems. (Jehl & Kirst, 1992, p. 95)

If the task is begun poorly, it will jeopardize and postpone future attempts to build interagency coalitions. Consequently, initial steps must be planned with utmost care. They must not fail. Planning should begin with a cadre of leaders who support the concept and who will work diligently to make the effort successful. Each agency or group that is invited to participate should be in good organizational health; that is, the agency/group should be operating effectively in meeting its own goals and objectives. An agency/group that is struggling to meet its own goals will have great difficulty taking on an interagency effort that requires sharing resources. The initial list of leaders to be included in this effort should include persons from the following types of groups, businesses, and agencies:

Social services
Employment services
Health services
Mental health and mental retardation
Social insurance
Juvenile justice
Community action groups
Clergy
Chamber of commerce
Service groups (e.g., Rotary, businesswomen's groups)
Town council
Police or sheriff's department
School district
Senior citizens

Other educational agencies
    Formal (vocational technical schools, community colleges,
        preschools, universities)
    Nonformal (Parent-Teacher Association or PTA, YMCA,
        day care centers, adult education centers)
Other community groups

Creating a Partnership

It is critical that these representatives view themselves as equal partners in this endeavor. To build trust from the very beginning, there must be an atmosphere of mutual respect and collegiality along with shared responsibility and control. The work of the collaborative team must ensure each agency's local autonomy and point of view, recognize each institution's limitations, and build on each institution's strengths.

For this partnership to work, the local school leader must serve as an advocate for an expanded school role in working with families and agency, business, and government leaders. Schools have steadily expanded their role in delivering comprehensive services to children and families over the past 100 years by offering a variety of health and social services, such as physical, optical, and dental examinations; immunizations; lunch and breakfast programs; and driver's training. The recent realization that the economic future and well-being of this country may very well be directly related to the intellectual and physical growth and development of the nation's children has caused both business and government to become more directly involved in education.

Although schools remain a central point where children and their families connect to the larger social and economic fabric of a community, it is understood that the impact the schools can make is limited. From birth to age 18, most children spend only 9% of their time actually in school. The other 91% of their lives is influenced by their families, their peers, their communities, and their exposure to various technologies, such as electronic news and entertainment media and video games.

Currently, the United States spends approximately $400 billion a year on public, K-12 education, and another $300 billion on human services on behalf of children. Even with the conservative estimate of a $700 billion annual investment in children, the nation's schools continue to be ineffective for nearly 40% of the students enrolled in them (Hodgkinson, 1993). The social potency of school-business-community-government partnerships is an essential ingredient for creating educational capacity for this lost 40%.

Underlying Assumptions

When beginning any collaborative effort, it is useful to develop a list of assumptions to guide the work. The assumptions listed below are in part borrowed from the Kentucky Family Resource and Youth Services Centers program, a state interagency collaborative project designed to "promote the flow of resources and support to families in ways [designed] to strengthen the functioning and enhance the growth and development of the individual members and the family unit" (Kentucky Cabinet for Human Resources, 1992).

- People are kind and want to do the right thing.
- People are very busy and often under a lot of pressure. If you provide them with some warm, human understanding and can show how working with you will make life easier for them, they will probably be more inclined to work with you.
- Establishing a cooperative working relationship is a process. Patience—up to a point—should pay off in the long run. You may not get all you need right away, but if you can start with small steps, the working relationship that you establish should get stronger. It is hoped that the fine-tuned working relationship that you eventually achieve will lead to the accomplishment of goals for all parties through exciting innovative efforts that will benefit all.
- Turf issues come with the territory and should be expected. They are a natural part of the process, especially until people who do not know each other well learn to trust one another.

- The individual with whom you are trying to work has knowledge and expertise and should be respected; this person could prove very helpful to you.

According to Deming (1986), "The aim of a team is to improve the input and the output of any stage" (p. 89). This team-building activity should be initiated at the first meeting of the group and should continue over several meetings. When clear underlying assumptions are established, groups are more productive and are able to withstand the inevitable conflicts that surface over time. Without these underlying assumptions the group may have difficulty maintaining constancy of purpose.

Creating Constancy of Purpose

Deming (1986) has identified two types of problems associated with constancy of purpose: problems of today and problems of tomorrow. *Problems of today* involve being sure that the present system is functioning at maximum effectiveness. *Problems of tomorrow* have to do with positioning the system to provide what will be needed in the future. Much of the school restructuring movement currently under way is focused on improving present educational capacity within the traditional educational system. Because creating constancy of purpose assumes that the system is continuously striving to deliver needed services for the future, it must address problems of the future.

We believe that this will require the creation of an expanded educational system that encompasses the collaborative efforts of communities, schools, judicial systems, government, and business. In Chapter 1 we introduced this concept, which we call Future School. As we have noted, the constancy of purpose for this effort will be to provide the following:

- Activities and services that will focus on improving the educational capacity of children and families
- Activities and services designed to improve the well-being of the community as a whole, not just the school community

- Activities and services designed to target prevention rather than traditional crisis intervention

In order to avoid reliance on outside funding sources, each participating group will attempt to redirect existing resources to avoid duplicating services and to expand the impact of the services delivered.

Team Building

The amount of trust established among groups will be directly related to the ability of the groups to work together as an effective team and the ability of each team member to communicate the work of his or her group to the agencies/groups represented. This process begins with the building of a strong team effort among the individuals represented and then supporting group members as they attempt to enhance efforts to build educational capacity within their respective agencies/groups. Teams must engage in processes that address personal differences, identify participants' unique strengths, develop team strengths, balance commitments to the project and commitments to their everyday jobs, and sustain long-term improvements. To focus on the primary goal of team formation, the group must develop a personal identity, establish positive relationships among team members, and identify with the purpose of the team. Using Deming's points, the team must develop a constancy of purpose, work collaboratively, and understand how the work of each team member contributes to the aim of the team.

Establishing a personal identity in the team forces members to work through issues related to membership inclusion, such as influence, control, mutual trust, getting along with one another, and mutual loyalty. Members need to understand how they fit into the team in order to develop a desire to remain on the team. Each member must be reassured that he or she will be heard and can influence the group's decisions. If members begin to perceive that one agency/group has more influence than another, the team will begin to break apart.

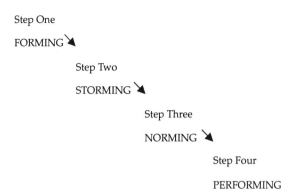

Figure 3.1. Developing Team Trust
SOURCE: Adapted from Scholtes (1988, pp. 6-4–6-8)

As a team works collaboratively, the team itself develops an identity of its own. It is this group identity that enables a team to work through the inevitable differences in opinion that occur over time.

Most team members want the team to work and are concerned with how the group will function. Will team meetings be formal or informal? What will happen when members disagree? Will the work of the team become political and perfunctory, or will the team deal with real, substantive problems? Will the members of the team like one another? What happens if they don't? If the team is able to establish answers that everyone can agree on, there is greater likelihood that the team will establish good working relationships among members.

Stages of Team Development

Scholtes (1988) has identified four stages of team growth: forming, storming, norming, and performing (see Figure 3.1). Particular feelings and behaviors are attached to each of these stages, as described below.

Forming

At the forming stage, group members are trying to figure out how to work together. Parameters of acceptable group behavior are being established. Group members rely on the group organizer to provide leadership in establishing these parameters. Questions related to the establishment of the group aim tend to dominate discussion during the time of group formation. It is not unusual for teams to spend time discussing lofty philosophical issues, identifying a multitude of problems related to their work, or attempting to identify information they will need to accomplish their task.

This is a critical stage. Team members will make judgments about whether they think the project is worthwhile, whether they think the members of the group will be productive, and whether the task at hand is realistic. According to Scholtes (1988), the feelings expressed by the group during the forming stage include the following:

- Excitement, anticipation, and optimism
- Pride in being chosen for the project
- Initial, tentative attachment to the team
- Suspicion, fear, and anxiety about the job ahead (p. 6-4)

It is during this stage that the group may begin to identify underlying assumptions on which they can formulate their constancy of purpose. During these early discussions, everyone should have an opportunity to contribute ideas, plans, and feelings. The following questions directed at various subgroups may be useful in helping a team get started.

Questions for an agency or group may include these:

- Where does the agency/group fit into the structure for building educational capacity for children?
- What services does the agency/group provide? How is the agency/group organized to deliver these services?
- How would educational capacity be affected if the agency/group did not exist?
- Does the agency/group have a long-range strategic plan?

Questions for the individual include the following:

- Where do you fit in your agency/group? What is your job? Who specifies what you do?
- Who supplies the information on which you design your work? How do you know it is the correct information?
- What are the results of your agency's/group's work?
- How do you know if you produce good results? How does your work affect children and/or the community's future?
- How do you know your services are effective? If your agency/group provides poor services, what happens? How do you know if you are meeting the needs of your clients?
- What are the standards used to determine effectiveness in your organization? Are these standards future oriented? Are they related to educational capacity or social capital?
- Who established the standards? How are standards revised?
- What annual reports are produced by your agency/group?

Questions concerning group/agency clientele might include these:

- To whom does the agency/group provide services?
- How does the agency/group know what clients' perceptions of the services are? How often are those perceptions monitored? How do those perceptions affect the organization's goals or standards?
- If the agency/group does not provide services directly to children, is it possible to determine the impact of the agency's/group's services on improving educational capacity, social capital, or the community's future? How?
- How does the authorizing body find out if the agency/group is delivering quality services?

The preceding questions can help the team to engage in productive dialogue that is essential for the development in members of a commitment to the group. Effective meetings should enable participants to share their individual levels of expertise and encourage members to share their insights. They should also be action and product oriented, and participants should be able to see how the work of one meeting relates to the next (Lindle, 1989).

Storming

At the storming stage, the difficulty of the task ahead begins to become more fully understood. Indeed, it often appears to be a formidable task at this point. Most human service agencies are part of larger bureaucracies with deep roots. Historically, collaboration among subgroups within the human service network has been less than ideal. Issues of turf, access to limited resources, and continuation of discrete programs are always sources of conflict among agencies. One of the reasons interagency collaboration and coordination are so complex is that they involve both agency collaboration problems and individual collaboration problems.

Examples of the dysfunctional history of collaboration among schools, community agencies, businesses, and government abound. Educators have traditionally attempted to maintain considerable distance from these other organizations. Educators prefer to focus on teaching rather than deal with the broader social context of families. Business leaders also have remained distant observers when it comes to questions regarding the schools. As long as there were enough qualified workers to fill jobs, most business involvement in schools was of a philanthropic nature. With businesses increasingly having difficulty finding workers with suitable knowledge, skills, and attitudes for employment, however, business leaders are taking a more serious look at how schools function. Government has been affected by an unstable economy in the past two decades. Local citizens are not willing to increase taxes to provide for additional services. Consequently, when school leaders attempt to bring together a group of people representing all of these diverse points of view, the participants bring with them their own narrow focuses on the issues and a lot of mistrust and skepticism about the success of collaboration.

How long the storming stage lasts may be directly related to the amount of mistrust the participants bring with them and each agency's/group's history of competence. Unless this mistrust can be overcome, the team will not succeed. It is important that the team leader be mindful of the need to take the necessary time to work through this stage before attempting to move on to the norming and performing stages.

According to Scholtes (1988), the feelings that surface during the storming stage include the following:

- Resistance to the task and to quality improvement approaches that differ from what each individual member is comfortable using
- Sharp fluctuations in attitude about the team and the project's chance of success
- Protectiveness about the prestige of one's own organization (p. 6-5)

As the team moves through this stage, it may be helpful if meetings are conducted at the offices of each agency/group represented. This practice enables team members to become familiar with other members' workplaces. The hosting agency/group could be in charge of the meeting and a major part of the agenda could focus on an overview of how that agency works—the organizational structure, funding sources, service populations—and its mission and vision for the future. Special emphasis should be given to how the hosting agency accomplishes its mission through collaboration with the team.

Such meetings also enable team members to become aware of the unique vocabularies associated with different groups. Eventually, the team members will develop a common language. These meetings would also offer team members the time they need to get to know one another on both formal and informal levels and allow for the necessity of working through negative group behaviors that Scholtes (1988) attributes to this stage, such as the following:

- Arguing among members even when they agree on the real issue
- Defensiveness and competition; factions and "choosing sides"
- Questioning the wisdom of those who selected this project and appointed the other members of the team
- Establishing unrealistic goals; concern about excessive work

- A perceived "pecking order"; disunity, increased tension, and jealousy (p. 6-6)

Norming

The real work of the team begins in the norming stage. Signs of the group reaching this level of team development include a general feeling of harmony within the group, a lack of tension, more laughter, and an easy give-and-take in the dialogue. At this point the team has developed a sense of team identity, collegiality, and common spirit. Feelings expressed by the group at the norming level include the following:

- A new ability to express criticism constructively
- Acceptance of membership in the team
- Acceptance of the team by the agencies/groups represented
- Recognition of the organizational capacity of participating agencies/groups
- Relief that it seems everything is going to work out (Scholtes, 1988, p. 6-6)

Performing

Now the team is ready to take action to deal directly with the team's goal or purpose. The length of time necessary for a team to get to this final stage cannot be predicted. Much of the process depends on the size of the group and the amount of mistrust group members bring with them initially. Groups that are forced to move too quickly into developing plans or identifying solutions to very difficult and complex interagency problems may be disappointed on three levels: (a) The solutions are superficial, (b) there is really little commitment to the implementation of changes, and (c) the group gets bogged down in controversy. The feelings evident at the performing stage include the following:

- Members having insights into personal and group processes, and better understanding of each other's strengths and weaknesses

- Members gaining an understanding of each organization's potential
- Satisfaction with the team's progress (Scholtes, 1988, p. 6-7)

Team members functioning at this stage exhibit close attachment to the team, are able to prevent or work through group problems, and are able to deal with constructive self-change.

Building Trust, Driving Out Fear

One of the primary objectives for this collaborative effort should be to enable each of the agencies/groups involved to be more successful in meeting its individual goals. According to Deming's second point, *adopting the new philosophy* means constantly checking that what drives action or behavior is an understanding of purpose and trust. For schools building links among business, government, and community, trust is tied to purpose if, and only if, all the groups and agencies can further their own goals by participating in inter-agency collaboration.

No longer can schools (or any other subgroup) protect turf from their primary clients, students and parents, or their secondary clients, the community. Primary clients now must be active participants in education. Teachers and administrators must seek their advice and use their own professional judgment to guide decision making with parents and students. Instead of being the objects of decisions, students and parents must become part of the process of decision making. When necessary, community agencies, organizations, and businesses should become involved in supporting student and parent decisions. Expertise from business, government, and community can be utilized by schools to further student and school success. Our whole thesis in this volume is that schooling can no longer be accomplished outside the mainstream of community, government, and business involvement. Resources are too scarce and educational capacity is too limited when schooling is attempted in a closed, isolated building distant from the support of its primary and secondary clienteles.

Suggested Meeting Record Format

Date _____   Location _____

Members present _____

_____

Meeting leader _____

Meeting facilitator _____

Meeting team builder _____

Meeting recorder _____

Agenda items—list each

Brief description   Summary of major points

Action taken

Next steps

Other topics—list each

[same format as agenda items]

Next meeting _____

Comments

Exhibit 3.1.

If any collaborative project is seen as an add-on, it can easily be "cut off" when agencies/groups change personnel or encounter internal problems or demands. If the collaborative effort works, each agency/group will fight to keep the collaboration going and, over time, it will be woven into the fabric of daily operations for each participating agency/group.

Building trust and driving out fear among group members can be facilitated through the way group meetings are organized. To help the team become more effective, four roles should be established: meeting leader, facilitator, team builder, and recorder. Team members should rotate into and out of the leader, facilitator, and builder roles. If the group is fortunate enough to have a permanent recording secretary, this function need not rotate. It may be possible to solicit a volunteer from the community to function in this role. If not, the person assuming the leader role may be able to

TABLE 3.1. Team Member Roles

Leader role
Prepare agenda.
Gather background materials.
Send meeting reminder.
Arrange for meeting space.
Start meeting on time.
At the meeting
Review agenda.
Follow agenda.
Make sure all members participate.
Summarize discussion.
Identify decision points.
Clarify actions taken.
Assist group in setting the agenda for the next meeting.
Facilitator role
Clarify when necessary.
Keep group on task.
Read group body language.
Facilitate dialogue and participation.
Listen.
End discussion when appropriate.
Test for consensus.
Team-builder role
Listen and watch team operation.
Report orally on strengths and areas to improve at the close of
  the meeting by responding to these two questions: What was
  good about this meeting? What could have been improved?
Recorder role
Use an agreed-on form to record meeting activities.
See that meeting summary is typed and sent to all team members.

bring a secretary with him or her. If neither of these ideas will work, then a member of the group should fill this function. Exhibit 3.1 shows a suggested format for recording the events of a meeting.

Each of the four roles has specific duties attached to it, and all four are critical to the successful operation of the team. Duties of each of the roles are outlined in Table 3.1.

Well-organized meetings build trust. The operations of the team are known. Everyone shares in the planning. Any fear that hidden agendas are driving the work of the group is dispelled. In a good meeting, team members gain confidence, take risks, push the dialogue into sensitive areas, think, and plan beyond existing parameters. To do this, each team member must fulfill his or her team role by doing the following:

- Accept responsibility for success of the meeting.
- Express opinions.
- Ask questions.
- Take positions and support them with details.
- Facilitate participation by all group members.
- Assist in reaching closure.
- Avoid dehumanizing comments.
- Reduce barriers to consensus building.
- Encourage dialogue from all team members.
- Be honest, respectful, and sensitive to others.
- Avoid digression.
- Set reasonable limits for discussion time.
- Assist in tension reduction.

Through removal of team members' fear, achievement of a transformed agency collaboration is maximized. As fear is driven out, the power of intrinsic motivation is released. Transformation cannot occur until the barriers created by the present system are overcome. Once these barriers are removed, the creative power of the team members will be released.

Perhaps the greatest barrier to achieving our transformed system is the lack of interagency/group collaboration and cooperation. Yet taking the first small steps toward this transformation requires participating agencies to have enough trust in the process and the participants of the group to overcome their present levels of mistrust and fear. These barriers will not be easily overcome.

Realistically, the objectives for the first year of work may be to drive out fear, build trust, become knowledgeable about the operation of each participating agency/group, and prepare a long-range strategic plan to guide team operations for years two through five,

TABLE 3.2.   Processes Used by Successful Teams

Clarify goals.
Develop a strategic plan.
Define roles.
Establish clear lines of communication.
Create an effective team.
Define decision-making procedures.
Achieve balanced participation.
Establish operational ground rules.
Understand group process.
Make decisions based on data.

SOURCE: Adapted from Scholtes (1988, pp. 6-10–6-21).

as well as begin collaborative endeavors. The first year's activities could be called *system building* as well as product oriented, because the focus is on laying the foundation for a megasystem that incorporates many subsystems.

Successful Teams

Currently, these subsystems operate as isolated systems of their own. Table 3.2 delineates the processes found in successful teams. In the first year, the new megasystem must clarify goals, develop an improvement plan, define roles, establish clear lines of communication, create an effective team, define decision procedures, achieve balanced participation, establish operational ground rules, gain an understanding of group processes, and make decisions based on data.

Clarify Goals

Early in the system transformation process, team members need to set both short- and long-term goals. Short-term goals should guide the work of the group over the first 6 to 12 months. Long-term goals will lead to the development of the transformed system. These may not be very specific at first, but they should serve to provide a sense of direction for the group. Short-term goals should serve to create the climate to enable the group to reach the performing level of team functioning and to develop a strategic long-range plan. The long- and short-term goals might be as follows:

LONG-TERM GOAL

- Create a new interagency/-group system designed to focus and connect services and programs to increase student achievement, enhance the quality of life of families, and improve economic growth and development of the community.

SHORT-TERM GOALS

- Develop an effective team.
- Become knowledgeable about operations of all subgroups represented on the team.
- Develop a common vocabulary.
- Create a long-range strategic plan.

If the team begins to switch directions, or flounders, argues frequently, exhibits frustration, or voices concern that the task at hand is too difficult to be accomplished, then the group should refocus and test commitment to both the short- and long-range goals. Many times, such problems are indicators that fear has not been driven out of the system. If they persist, the group may need to engage in additional team-building activities to stabilize the group and to refocus on the long-range goal.

Develop a Strategic Plan

The long-range strategic plan should be developed during the last half of the first year and should guide the work of the group for the next four or five years. The plan should include the development of a flowchart that outlines step-by-step activities designed to enable the system to meet its goals. (We will outline the steps to be taken in the development of this long-range strategic plan in Chapter 4.) The plan can then serve as a basis for the necessary professional development for each subagency/subgroup to implement the plan. Agencies may find it useful to coordinate some of the professional development across agencies/groups. This would be beneficial in enabling staff from a variety of agencies/groups to get to know one another and to expand the level of trust across the transformed system.

The team may want to consider engaging a planning facilitator to assist in generating this plan, because the development of a long-range strategic plan requires technical skills. If this expertise resides within one of the collaborating agencies/groups, it may be possible to get the agency/group to assign the planner to the project. Without a facilitator, the team could run into obstacles, such as not being sure what should be done next, identifying activities without clear understanding of why those activities are important, and not being able to sequence the coordination of activities across agencies/groups.

Define Roles

In addition to defining roles within the team, team members should clearly define their roles within their sending agencies/groups for other members. This role clarification should include specifying functions related to authority and procedures for policy setting, communication, reporting mechanisms, resource allocation, and information sharing. This process should promote the development of trust within and across agencies/groups represented on the team.

Establish Clear Lines of Communication

The person in the role of team builder can assist in making sure that the team utilizes effective communication strategies during meetings. Characteristics of an effective communicator include clarity of speech, active listening, the ability to be direct and succinct, avoiding interruption, and sharing information through a variety of techniques. Scholtes (1988) describes five types of statements that promote communication:

- Sensing statements ("I don't hear any disagreements with the point. Do we all agree?")

- Thinking statements ("There seems to be a correlation between the number of agencies involved with a family and the
  level of family dysfunction.")
- Feeling statements ("I'm disappointed that we haven't been
  able to collaborate more effectively in the past.")
- Statements of intentions ("My comment was not a criticism,
  it simply reflects the way things are.")
- Statements of actions ("Let's conduct a needs assessment to
  determine if the service is one the community wants.") (p. 6-14)

Effective communication is blocked when participants feel that
they cannot express how they really feel, some group members
dominate the conversation, comments are not responded to, or
opinions are presented as facts. The level of communication relates
directly to the level of trust within the group.

Create an Effective Team

One way to measure the effectiveness of a team is to determine
if there is a dramatic difference in the openness, candor, and ease of
communication in conversations held directly before and after the
formal meeting. If the team is operating effectively, the conversation
in the formal meeting will be directed toward agenda items, but it
should still reflect the same level of trust as the conversations before
and after the meeting. If it does not, this means that some members
have developed high levels of trust, but the total group is still
inhibited by fear. The team needs to identify and drive out the
sources of this fear.

Define Decision-Making Procedures

Group decision-making procedures should appear on the agenda of one of the team's earliest meetings. Unless these procedures
are formally discussed and agreed on, the group will tend to con-
cede to positions taken by forceful group members, rely on majority
vote, or allow a decision to be made without input or buy-in from
all group members. Preferably, the group should use consensus as
the primary group decision-making practice.

Whenever possible, decisions should be based on data. Data-based decision making is a hallmark of TQE. The trick here is to be sure that all relevant data from all of the contributing agencies are made available to the team. (See Table 2.1 for a list of relevant data and sources.) Every effort should be made to avoid decision making based on opinion rather than fact. The role of team builder or facilitator could include monitoring the data used in decision making.

Achieve Balanced Participation

Balanced participation in a cross-agency/-group team is difficult to achieve. Just as there is a pecking order within an organization, there is a pecking order among agencies/groups in a community. For example, a representative from the sheriff's office may be perceived to have more clout than a representative from the juvenile justice office, or vice versa.

Acting as an enabler to be sure that all members of the team have equal opportunity to speak is a major role of the team facilitator. By rotating this responsibility among all team members, the team sees to it that each participant has an opportunity to become sensitive to the internal dynamics of the team. Over time, all members of the team will help to promote total group dialogue. Unless balanced participation is achieved, a few members of the team will dominate the discussion, and the agencies they represent may tend to dominate the direction of the work. Over time, those agencies/groups that feel that their voices have not been heard will loose interest and commitment to the objectives of the effort.

Maintaining balanced group participation requires giving and receiving constructive feedback. Scholtes (1988) makes the following recommendations for giving and receiving feedback.

GIVING FEEDBACK

- Be descriptive.
- Don't use labels.
- Don't exaggerate.
- Don't be judgmental.
- Speak for yourself.

- Talk first about yourself, not about the other person.
- Phrase the issue as a statement, not a question.
- Restrict your feedback to things you know for certain.
- Help people hear and accept your compliments when giving positive feedback.

RECEIVING FEEDBACK

- Breathe deeply.
- Listen to what is being said.
- Ask clarifying questions.
- Acknowledge the feedback.
- Accept valid points.
- Take time to be sure you understood what was said. (p. 6-24)

Establish Operational Ground Rules

No one has time to participate in meetings where the operational ground rules have not been established. Part of what is being worked out in the forming, storming, and norming stages of the team are the ground rules. All participants have a right to know what is expected regarding length of meetings, how agendas are built, how conflicts will be resolved, and what is acceptable and unacceptable behavior in the group. Most important, every meeting should have an established outcome. When people leave a meeting, they should know what is expected of them between meetings and what the next meeting will accomplish (Lindle, 1989). The ground rules should be reviewed from time to time to be sure they still reflect the desires of the group. The ground rules should be shared with each contributing agency/group, so that everyone has a general understanding of how the team functions.

Understand Group Process

Another topic that should be addressed in one of the first few meetings is the whole area of group process. If all participants in the group have a sound understanding of how groups function, and if they are sensitive to reading both verbal and nonverbal cues, then everyone can assist in keeping the group on task and productive. For instance, it is important to deal with underlying issues related to a topic being discussed. Ignoring issues will not make them go away; they will simply surface again later on, and they could sabotage the effort. Generally, before a concern is expressed verbally there are nonverbal cues present. Failure to recognize nonverbal signs of resistance, lack of understanding, and unhappiness can inhibit the progress of the group. The team builder or the facilitator can be enormously helpful in guiding team members through group process issues.

Make Decisions Based on Data

Of all the requirements for a successful team, this may be the most important. It will be through the use of data analysis that the team will be able to determine whether problems are related to a faulty system or to individuals within the system. Deming (1993) estimates that 85% of all problems are system problems, not people problems, yet we tend to blame the people in a system rather than the system itself when troubles arise.

In attempting to create a transformed system that extends beyond the traditional parameters of the school, the effectiveness of each of the subsystems will have to be scrutinized. Team members must insist on having all relevant data before making decisions, and they should be certain that the data they review are related to the root of a problem, not just a symptom. For example, attendance, retention, and dropout data, although informative, do not tell us the root problem in schools; they are indicators that point to student motivation and success, which might be related to family dysfunction, which in turn might be related to community economy. So, in exploring the issue of student achievement in our interagency/intergroup team, we may need to collect data from many different agencies. (See Chapter 2 for lists of possible data sources and standards for building an interagency information system.)

Key Terms and Concepts

Balanced participation. Representative input from a variety of groups and individuals in which no one person or group is allowed to dominate the process or suppress another person or group's views or perceptions.

Building trust. The idea that a state of acceptance and confidence in constancy of future actions can be created among individuals, groups, or agencies through purposive planning and other human relations activities.

Ground rules. The protocols to be used formulating a strategic plan through consensus and trust building.

Norming stage. That demarcation in the development of team building that includes an easy, nondefensive give-and-take of ideas or feelings.

Partnership. A collaborative relationship, usually based on collegial actions that permit team building.

Performing stage. That demarcation in the development of team building that includes the gaining of deep insights into the agendas and problems of the partners or the agencies they represent.

Planning facilitator. A person with skills in group dynamics who assists individuals in the development of a strategic plan by minimizing conflict and maximizing the grounds for consensus.

Storming stage. The team-building stage that focuses on tensions between individual and group identities.

Strategic plan. A type of thinking that, once put to paper, identifies long-range goals, surrounding contextual data and trends, and a mission to be accomplished or a position to be reached over time.

Team building. The deliberate act of creating a common interest to act on a shared cause or set of goals by two or more persons.

Turf issues. Problems that are confined to a geographic or political territory by one party who refuses to allow others to engage them.

References

Deming, W. E. (1986). *Out of the crisis.* Cambridge: MIT Center for Advanced Engineering Study.

Deming, W. E. (1993, May 11-14). Remarks made at a conference on quality assurance, Dallas, TX.

Hodgkinson, H. (1993). American education: The good, the bad, and the task. *Phi Delta Kappan, 74,* 619-623.

Jehl, J., & Kirst, M. (1992). Getting ready to provide school-linked services: What schools must do. *Future of Children, 2*(1), 95-106.

Kentucky Cabinet for Human Resources. (1992). *Family Resource and Youth Services Center coordinator's guide.* Frankfort: Author.

Lindle, J. C. (1989). Take parents seriously, and they'll get seriously involved. *Executive Educator, 11*(11), 24-25.

Scholtes, P. R. (1988). *The team handbook.* Madison, WI: Joiner Associates.

Getting the Partners' Act Together

The current system of public education in the United States may be operating as well as it can. According to Hodgkinson (1993), the current system of schools provides about 20% of students with an education that meets world-class standards, about 40% of our children receive a marginally effective education, and 40% face failure. Albert Shanker (1992), spokesman for the American Federation of Teachers, simply says, "We have reached the limits of our traditional model of education, and the whole system requires rethinking and reworking" (p. 4). Because schooling is intimately connected to other government and community functions, we ought to note that seriously restructuring or transforming of schools cannot be done alone. It will require interagency collaboration.

The Nature of Interagency Collaboration

Interagency collaboration has long roots in the United States. In earlier times, when there was less family mobility and communities were smaller, persons "in need" could rely on their extended families and networks of neighbors and church groups for support. This old-fashioned system involved no human service bureaucracy, eligibility criteria, application process, or service monitoring. It simply recognized human need and tried to provide services or direct families to places where they could receive help. Generally, the assistance was not meant to be long-term in nature. The original idea of assistance to families was to help them get over a rough time, to help them to get back on their feet.

The expectation that short-term support should be sufficient to enable families to resolve immediate problems and return to a status of self-sufficiency no longer holds. The present situation, as described by the program coordinator of one agency, is this:

> The problems facing families today are of a completely different magnitude than those of the past. This is not a case of simply losing a job and needing some assistance until you find the next one. The problems today deal with substance abuse, physical abuse, addiction, and poverty. These are complex problems and require complex solutions. Family members are not saying to their children, I love you and we will make it through these tough times. Rather, the adults appear to be totally overwhelmed by the situation and abandon the emotional needs of their children. (P. Roberts, Family Resource Youth Services Centers, Fayette County Schools, Lexington, KY, personal communication, June 1993)

The creation of a new interagency collaborative effort is based on the belief that it should be possible to create a service delivery model that promotes a public attitude for self-sufficiency through short-term intervention, as opposed to the present system, which provides lifetime, even intergenerational, support for a growing number of children and families. Many agree that the place to begin to break the lifelong dependency cycle is with children. It is also clear that the problems children bring to school are problems of the home, the community, and the larger society. The schools did not create the problems children bring to the schoolhouse door, and the schools, in far too many cases, do little to help provide solutions.

Schools have traditionally been places where the educational delivery process has remained constant and isolated. Children differ in their readiness to succeed in the system, but the system remains constant. Consequently, schools have become highly efficient sifting and sorting mechanisms, in which children who come to school prepared are the ones who succeed. Research indicates that one of the key elements in a child's success in school is the child's having a strong, nurturing relationship with an adult (Coleman, 1987; Comer, 1980). If this is true, the community must find ways to provide that strong, nurturing relationship when it is missing from a child's immediate family. Doing less almost certainly assures that the child will become part of the 40% for which the present system fails. In Chapter 3, we outlined a process that school administrators could use to form a nucleus for a collaborative, interagency system made up of schools, business, government, and the community in order to create our vision of Future School. We suggested that time and attention be devoted to developing the team that would construct the strategic long-range plan for this expanded interagency system. In this chapter, we will focus on the specific steps the team should take in constructing this plan.

Establishing Realistic Strategic Long-Range Plans

The purpose of a strategic long-range plan is to concentrate the resources available on mutually determined, measurable outcomes. Such a plan is built on the assumption that the aim of the system is clearly understood by all, and that this aim guides the work of the system. By continually focusing and refocusing on this aim, the system maintains a constancy of purpose over time. The system then becomes "a network of interdependent components that work together to try to accomplish the aim of the system" (Deming, 1993, p. 50). To fulfill an aim in the idealized sense conceptualized by Deming, everyone in the system benefits. There are no losers.

General summaries of the cost of public education for grades K-12 indicate that we spend about $5,000 annually per child. If the $300 billion spent on human services to support children is added, it could be argued that a conservative estimate of an additional $2,000 per child is available to serve children's needs (National Center for Educational Statistics, 1992). Given approximately $7,000 per child, per year, can an interagency, collaborative system be successful in providing more than 25% of the children in a community with an education that meets world-class standards? Stated another way, given $7,000 per year, can this new, expanded educational system reduce the failure rate to somewhat less than 40%? We think the answer to both questions is a resounding yes, but it will require the creation of a new system of public education. It will require Future School, as introduced in Chapter 1.

The current public educational system in the United States was never designed to be effective with 100% of our children. Shanker (1992), Hodgkinson (1993), Kozol (1991), Sarason (1990), Steffy (1993), and other researchers believe that, unless the United States acts quickly to redesign, restructure, and reconceptualize public education, this country will lose its position as a world leader. Some have predicted that we are quickly leaving behind both the industrial age and the information age. On the horizon is the intellectual age, where "learning has become the strategically central enterprise for national economic strength" (Perelman, 1992, p. 20).

Deming's (1993) conceptualization for improving a system rests on the Shewhart cycle. The steps in this cycle include planning, carrying out the plan, studying the results, making changes based on the results, and beginning the cycle again. Stated in its simplest form, it means: Plan, do, study, and act. In this chapter we will apply this model to show how school leaders can design an effective, collaborative school improvement process. The process begins with a needs assessment.

Many of Deming's 14 points are incorporated in the fundamental principles of the strategic planning process as defined by Bill Cook (1990). Strategic planning entails the following:

- A voluntary commitment to generate rational decisions about the deployment of resources toward fixed goals and priorities
- An obligation to achieve measurable results translated ultimately into performance standards for those individuals responsible for implementing the plan
- A prescription that is formulated by the combined expertise within the system
- A consensus plan derived through the application of participative management

Strategic planning unleashes creativity from throughout the system, sparks new enthusiasm for excellence, and guarantees progress without the artificial limitations of budget, because the planning begins and ends with ideas and aspirations.

There is also an assumption undergirding the strategic long-range planning process that attaining new goals means changing the system. The implication here is that problems in attaining desired results are generally system problems, and not people problems.

Needs Assessment

Three overall questions should guide the design of the needs assessment:

- What are the problems we are trying to solve?
- What are the current resources available for solving them?
- Is there a better way to use available resources to solve them?

The first step in the needs assessment process is to assemble all the information available on the status of children and services in the community (see Table 2.1 for a complete list of data sources). These data should be disaggregated in several ways, such as by race, income level, or age, to provide a better description of the community.

Additional data can be obtained through a variety of more informal data-collection techniques. For example, planners can do the following:

- Invite a group of students who have dropped out of school to attend a team meeting and talk about factors that contributed to their decisions to leave school.
- Identify families who use three or more of the social services within the community and interview them regarding their needs.
- Develop a community survey to assess what services are currently being utilized.
- Survey the business community regarding their current skill needs for employees and projected skill needs for the future.

The second step in the needs assessment process is to document the public and private services currently available in the community. This assessment began with the trust-building phase for those agencies/groups represented on the team. Now the information-collection process is expanded to include the total community.

In addition to data about services/programs available, information about the effectiveness of individual services/programs is also important. For instance, perhaps the local school district offers parenting classes, but few of the parents of dysfunctional students ever attend. Or perhaps the community has several private day care facilities, but families without transportation cannot take advantage of them. Or perhaps the unemployment agency serves 10% of the workers in the community, but 15% have been unemployed for longer periods of time than are covered by the benefits. This phase of the needs assessment process should also provide data on the staffing levels of the service agencies and information about caseloads.

After all data have been analyzed, they should serve as a description of "what is" in the system. The next step is to determine "what should be." In 1992, Roger Kaufman assisted the Florida Department of Education in the development of a book titled *Needs Assessment for Florida Schools*, which details a step-by-step process for conducting a needs assessment. The process addresses three levels of needs assessment: the mega-, macro-, and microlevels. Kaufman defines megalevel needs assessment as the assessment of society needs, macrolevel as school needs, and microlevel as classroom needs. In applying this process to the creation of Future School, the megalevel would entail the community, government, business, and the school. The microlevel would then apply to the individual agencies/groups within the community. By identifying current results and desired results at the three levels, it is possible to determine the gap between what is and what should be and then to make some determination about what practices to keep, what to add, what to drop, and why.

It is important to note that needs indicate gaps in results, not gaps in resources or methods. Kaufman (1992) refers to this distinction between means and ends as a critical success factor. Very often, we confuse means with ends or results. For example, a social worker is successful in working with 20 of her current caseload of 50 families.

TABLE 4.1. Needs Assessment: Examples of Means and Ends

Means

    Additional staff

    More money

    More time

    Newsletters

    Meals on Wheels

    Chapter I

    PTA

    Social services

    Head Start

Ends

    All high school graduates with demonstrated high achievement

    Full employment

    Growing community economy

    All parents supporting schools

    Students entering school ready to learn

The desired result is success with 50 families. The need is increased success with more families. The need is not for an additional social worker; that is a means, not a desired result or end. This distinction between means and needs is critical to the success of any planning effort. See Table 4.1 for a list of possible means and desired ends.

A number of means may be considered in achieving the desired result. Kaufman (1992) suggests that one of the reasons we are having difficulty in education is that we often confuse means and needs. Sometimes we decide on a solution before we understand the needs.

If the needs assessment process includes a questionnaire, it is important to consider the following points, as delineated by the Florida Department of Education (1992, p. 53; used by permission):

- Make certain that the questions are about results, not about processes or inputs.
- Ask about perceptions of gaps in results for both dimensions: what is and what should be.
- Assure validity and reliability of questions.

- Make questionnaires long enough to get reliable responses, but short enough that people will actually respond.
- Use an approach that makes it clear to respondents exactly what is wanted. People usually don't want to write long answers, so a checklist will reduce their burden while making the questionnaire easier to score.
- Don't ask questions that reveal, directly or indirectly, a bias. Don't use the data collection vehicle to set up the responses you really want.
- Ask several questions about each dimension or issue. Ask about each concern in different ways to assure reliability in the responses. Basing any decision on answers to one question is risky.
- Try out the data collection instrument on a sample group to identify problems in meaning, coverage, and scorability. Revise it as required.

When collecting performance (or "hard") data, do the following:

- Make certain the data collected relate to issues for which you want answers.
- Assure yourself that the data you use are collected correctly and that the methods used for gathering it and reporting it are free of bias.
- Assure yourself that the data are based upon enough observations to make them reliable, not a one-shot happening.
- Make certain that the data can be independently verified and cross-checked.

The final step in the needs assessment process is the most difficult. This involves analyzing the data and presenting the analysis in such a way that it leads to the needs to be addressed in the planning process. This may require further information about services/programs relating to their effectiveness and use.

This step should include both internal and external analysis. An internal analysis includes the identification of the strengths and weaknesses of the present system in addition to internal trends that will have an effect on the system. Examples of internal trends could include a plant closing or a major expansion of an industry to include three shifts. A plant closing may trigger the need for the development of new adult training programs. The expansion of a plant to three shifts may create the need for the development of a 24-hour day care program.

It is important to remember that the primary purposes for this endeavor are to improve the status of children, increase educational capacity, and maximize potential for happy, healthy, contributing members of society. During this data collection and analysis phase, one of the major objectives should be to collect as much information about children as possible.

Data from the school system should assist in determining what happens to students over time within the school system. The following questions could guide this data collection process:

- At what point did students currently graduating from the system enter the district's schools?
- What is the present mobility factor at each school?
- Are there exit interviews to determine why students move or drop out?
- Do the exit interviews include specific questions about both educational and social conditions that might influence a student to move or drop out?
- What is the mobility factor between schools in the district?
- What is the orientation process for new students entering the system?
- What is the orientation process for parents of these new students?
- How are high expectations for parent and student involvement and accountability established and communicated?
- How are parents and students mentored during the first few months in the community?
- Does the school provide parent support groups? If so, at what level and for what purpose?
- What type of two-way communication system has the school established with parents? Does it include voice mail?
- How are parents made aware of the successes students are having in school?

- What support mechanisms does the school use to assist students when they encounter problems?
- Does the school have a student assistance program?
- What are the dropout, attendance, and retention rates for each level of the system?
- Are follow-up studies conducted on dropouts?
- Are follow-up studies conducted for transition from high school?

A concurrent study should be conducted for the business community to determine the status of families over the same 12-year period. Questions dealing with the business aspects of families could include the following:

- What are the growth patterns within the community over the past 10 to 15 years?
- What are the income levels of those employed within the community at the present time?
- What have been the yearly percentages of unemployment over the past 10 to 15 years?
- What new businesses have started within the community over the past 10 to 15 years?
- What businesses have closed within the community?
- What types of businesses have opened and closed during the past 5 years?

There are similar questions for assessing government along these lines:

- What legislation has been passed at the local and state levels within the past 5 years that supports the status of families and children?
- What legislation is pending that promotes the status of families and children?
- On what platform did government officials run? How does that relate to community economic growth and development?
- What communication patterns currently exist among various levels of local, state, and national government?

- What issues do persons in government positions feel are most important?

Finally, questions for human services should be addressed:

- How are the services delivered by various agencies currently coordinated?
- What cross-agency communication mechanisms currently exist?
- On what data does each agency determine successful operation?
- Does each agency have a strategic plan? Is a copy available?
- What services are currently available within the community?
- What new services have been added during the past 5 to 10 years?
- What is the level of state and federal funding for each of these agencies?
- Does each agency have an advisory board? Who is on it?

The external analysis includes the identification of those forces/events that are taking place outside the present system that could have an impact on the present system. State budget reductions, federal revamping of the welfare system, and the implementation of national health care reform are all examples of external forces that must be taken into consideration in the planning process.

Mission Statement

Developing a mission statement for this new system is a formidable task. A mission statement represents the essence of a system's purpose. It clarifies the aim of the enterprise and provides the target that will help to maintain the system's constancy of purpose. The trick here will be to develop a mission statement for this collaborative effort that provides every contributing agency/group with an opportunity to grow and develop, one that promotes a win/win collaborative environment, and one that supports rather than impedes the attainment of each participant's mission.

The mission statement should empower everyone in the expanded system to assume responsibility for the ultimate success of the system. This means that everyone will be able to see how their work relates to the work of others and how, collectively, the work of the subunits contributes to the overall success of Future School. Further, the mission represents a commitment, a pledge, a road map against which decisions can be weighed and actions determined. The mission should assist the leadership within each subgroup to establish priorities and objectives.

In a short, concise paragraph, the mission statement conveys a statement of purpose, describes the uniqueness of the system, and establishes a value-laden commitment. It is the keystone on which a strategic long-range plan is established. This statement should answer the following three questions:

- What is the unique role of this collaborative effort?
- What is our vision?
- What do we hope to accomplish for our community?

Some guidelines for developing a mission statement include the following:

- Identify the community's major stakeholder in the development of the mission statement.
- Formulate a plan that involves these major stakeholders in the strategic planning process.
- If the group developing the strategic plan is different from the initial advisory group that initiated plans for this community collaborative effort, devise a mechanism to keep the advisory group informed about the progress of the planning process.
- Focus on areas of agreement, not areas of disagreement.
- Keep the statement short, simple, and easy to understand and remember.

After the statement is approved, everyone involved in the collaborative effort should refer to it frequently during the decision-making process, as policies and programs are formulated. Later, they should review the mission statement periodically to be sure it still reflects the vision of where the system wants to go.

Developing an
Interagency Improvement Plan

After the mission statement has been developed, it is time to establish the interagency improvement plan. After the interagency improvement plan is completed, it would be wise to share this plan with the staff of each of the contributing agencies/groups, to provide awareness and to develop agency buy-in. One way to facilitate buy-in is to ask each staff member in each affected agency to review the plan, make suggestions for improvement, raise questions and concerns, and ultimately accept the plan by signing a form and returning it to his or her agency head. This review will ensure that each person has had input into the process. One of the most difficult obstacles to overcome in this type of collaborative effort is the belief on the part of individuals employed by the various agencies that their jobs are in jeopardy. Once assured that this is not so, they are much more open to the idea of collaboration. After the interagency plan is accepted, each contributing agency should develop an agency action plan to show how the agency will contribute to the overall collaborative effort.

The interagency improvement plan must include goals and objectives and plans to document results. Many of the data compiled as part of the needs assessment can serve as baseline data. After a period of time—for instance, two years—these baseline data can be compared with new baseline data, thereby documenting change over time.

The Planning Office for the Fayette County School System in Lexington, Kentucky, has developed an 11-step process for determining priorities for action related to improvement plans. These steps, reprinted below by permission of the Planning Office, could be used to determine the priorities for the community interagency improvement plan or for the action plans of the contributing agencies/groups. This process should be used for each suggested strategy. (Note: The first two steps may have been completed during the needs assessment process.)

Step 1: Define the issue/problem/need.

- List facts about the present state/current status of the issue/problem. Avoid defining the problem in terms of opinions, solutions, or lower order problems.
- Determine the goal or desired state. Remember, the issue/problem/need is defined as the difference between where you currently are and where you have determined you need to be.
- State the issue/problem/need.

Step 2: Gather information about the issue/problem/need.

- Gather facts about potential contributing factors; attitudes of parents, students, teachers, business leaders, and community members; demographic data; student and family profile data, issues that need to be considered; and so on.
- Gather information/research about what has been effective in dealing with this issue/problem/need.

Step 3: Diagnose the problem, analyze obstacles that may keep you from getting to your desired state.

- Analyze strengths and opportunities: Gather information about everything that will facilitate achieving your goal.
- Analyze weaknesses and obstacles: Gather information about everything that will restrain you from achieving your goal.
- Assign importance weights to each force (one to three works well). Evaluate the relative weights of the facilitating and restraining forces.
- Develop strategies for enhancing the most critical facilitating forces, and for reducing the impact of the most critical restraining forces.

Step 4: Find general solutions.

- Based on all of the information gathered and analyzed, brainstorm potential solutions.

Step 5: Discuss and evaluate the solutions.

- Determine as a group what criteria will be used for evaluating the solutions.
- Discuss the merits of each listed solution on the basis of the established criteria.
- As a group, rank the solutions from best to poorest.

*Step 6: Choose solutions that will
be implemented through a plan.*

- Determine the following for each solution chosen:
    Rationale/background information: What information/ research supports this solution?
    Statement of activity and time line: What specifically are you going to do, and what are the targeted beginning and ending dates?
    Leadership/responsibility: Who is responsible for making sure that the action plan is implemented, and what will be the responsibilities of staff members in carrying out this plan?
    Resources: Will this activity require additional space, training for staff, or funding for materials or other resources? How will these needs be met?
    Evaluation: What criteria will be used to measure progress? What is the plan for collecting information to determine results?
    Communication plan: What is your plan for informing others about this activity and the results you achieve?

Step 8: Present completed plans.

- Each agency/group involved should provide an orientation for the entire staff so that everyone understands how his or her work contributes to the aim.

Step 9: Implement plans.

- A specific person should be assigned responsibility for monitoring the implementation of the plan. This individual should prepare periodic reports to document progress.
- Persons working to implement the plan should have opportunities to meet and talk to discuss issues and problems and propose modifications to address these concerns.

Step 10: Evaluate results.

- Program evaluation should include both formative and summative measures. This evaluation should include services provided, resources used, service delivery mechanisms, organizational processes, participant characteristics, and progress toward meeting program objectives.
- Formative evaluation measures can include consumer satisfaction surveys, resource analysis, service statistics, participant records, and documentation of how the program functions in relation to need, action to address the need, and benefits to participants.
- Summative evaluation procedures should attempt to address the effects of the service on people's lives, particularly those of children and families. Attempts should be made to collect these data yearly. In addition, there should be an attempt to collect community impact data and to conduct cost-benefit analysis and collect cost-effectiveness data.

Step 11: Summarize and communicate progress over time.

- Formal progress reports should be published periodically. This could be done on a yearly or biyearly basis. Agencies may want to relate reports to their own funding cycles.
- These formal reports should serve as a basis for updating the strategic long-range plan. The summative report for one time period becomes part of the needs assessment data for the next period.

Agency/Group Resources

The resources of all facets of the community can be utilized to meet the aim of coordinating the flow of these resources to support children and families in ways to improve the academic achievement of students and strengthen the functioning, growth, and development of all members of the family unit. In developing plans to achieve this aim, agencies/groups may want to consider some of the activities listed below, which are adapted from the state implementation plan of the Kentucky Family Resource and Youth Services Centers. This list of suggested activities is not intended to be complete or all-inclusive; it is meant only to stimulate ideas.

Suggestions for Possible Activities

PARENTS AS PARTNERS

- Train volunteer parents to be child-care providers in order to allow a program design of sharing of child-care service.
- Identify activities through which parents may learn about or participate in all aspects of child-care services.
- Organize parent support groups (with child-care provided).
- Prepare and/or obtain booklets on family issues.
- Deliver training for new and expectant mothers.
- Organize in-home visits by parent educators who offer child development information, suggest practical ways for parents to encourage their child's development, and monitor the child's progress to ensure that health problems or developmental delay can be addressed as early as possible.
- Provide information on adult instruction courses available in the community.
- Provide adult literacy training.
- Provide vocational education counseling and assessment.
- Create programs for employment skill development.

HEALTH SERVICES,
REFERRAL TO HEALTH SERVICES, OR BOTH

- Provide school-site preventive health care and referral.

- Conduct health risk appraisal and follow-up counseling.
- Update school health and family life curriculum.
- Develop speaker's bureau for health care issues.
- Assist local library in developing a resource center for health care print and nonprint materials.
- Identify and secure videos pertaining to health care and organize a lending library.

DRUG/ALCOHOL ABUSE COUNSELING

- Coordinate in-school education and awareness presentations for students, staff, and families.
- Assist in the establishment of a student assistance program within the school setting.
- Develop and implement a community education and public awareness program to address youth-specific needs and problems.

FAMILY CRISIS AND MENTAL HEALTH COUNSELING

- Develop a resource network for the identification of service providers for specific crisis issues with complete service referrals and follow-up procedures (e.g., financial assistance; emergency housing, food, and clothing; child and spouse abuse services; traveler's aid; truancy).
- Determine inpatient and outpatient resources for youth and family.
- Assist in monitoring youth and families with identified psychiatric needs if qualified staff is available.
- Assist with the transition of youth from inpatient treatment to the community school placement.
- Secure training for school personnel, youth, and families in suicide prevention education.

JUVENILE JUSTICE ISSUES

- Develop a program to coordinate with local courts, attorneys, court-designated workers, the Department of Social Services, and school-level decision-making councils to provide early and appropriate interventions for youth with behavioral problems.

- Design a process to facilitate the reentry of youth into the school system from residential treatment, private child care, and out-of-district placements.

COMMUNITY

- Develop a plan to attract youth to community recreation facilities.
- Provide an after-school or out-of-school program to accommodate the recreation needs of youth in the community.
- Create a network of government, industry, and business willing to allow youth an opportunity for volunteer activities.
- Develop a community mentoring program to link students in need of adult role models with community leaders.

BUSINESS

- Develop business and industry internships for middle and high school students to expand their awareness about opportunities in the world of work.
- Facilitate networking between the business community and the school community to utilize the educational facilities and staff for employee skill updates.
- Provide for off-site classes for high school students utilizing the training facilities of business and industry within the community.
- Involve business leaders in assessing student progress through participation in student portfolio review and serving as members of student-juried exhibitions.
- Create a local interagency/group foundation to receive donations and solicit grants to support the work of the collaboration.
- Sponsor cross-agency employee exchanges to facilitate mutual growth and understanding.

GOVERNMENT

- Sponsor focused discussion groups on issues related to public policy and legislation.
- Prepare videotapes of local and area government officials discussing their positions on local, state, and national issues.
- Prepare draft legislation to improve cross-agency/-program collaboration and communication.

PRIVATE COMMUNITY GROUPS AND SERVICES

- Develop mechanisms to facilitate regular communication with all constituencies attempting to serve the community.
- Organize an annual event to showcase private community groups and services.

OTHER

- Seek funds to support a position within the community to act as a clearinghouse of all community programs and services that have an impact on the status of children and families.
- Develop community commitment to serve the needs of all children.

Local Reputation

Every community has a local reputation. Generally, that reputation is tied to the quality of life within the community, and this quality of life is also related to the community's growth factor. The higher the quality of life, the greater the possibility that the community will grow and flourish. A significant component of a community's quality of life is the status of youth and children. By looking at the status of children within the schools, within the community, and within families, it is not difficult to define a community's reputation. The status of children is not affected only by the school system, or the family system, or the human services system. These are all subparts of a larger community system that make up Future School. Improving the schools means improving the larger system that affects children. School improvement is linked to community improvement. Community improvement is linked to community reputation. When the route taken to reach school improvement is community improvement, everyone benefits.

Producing school improvement through community improvement does not require every facet of the community to become believers in this approach, but it does require the creation of an energized critical mass. The concept of critical mass originated in physics. It is based on the premise that once a certain state is achieved, it becomes self-sustaining. If a community can energize a critical mass of agencies/groups to approach community improvement as improvement of the lives of children and families, and these processes become self-sustaining, the reputation of the community will continuously improve over time. Although many subgroups within communities have been working to enhance the communities' reputations, few efforts have focused on improving the lives of children as the vehicle to accomplish this task. We are suggesting that approach.

The concept of critical mass has been applied to the social sciences as well as the physical sciences. Research related to critical mass in the social sciences seems to suggest that it is reached when 5% to 20% of the people become involved, energized, and believing in a particular change. For most change efforts involving people, about 12% appears to be the key proportion for reaching critical mass. It seems to us that it should not be too difficult to find the critical mass of 12% of the leaders within a community who would want to approach community improvement through improving the lives of children.

Accepting this challenge does not mean being perfect in all that we do. However, it does mean always maintaining a "go-for-it" attitude, self-reflection, openness to new ideas, and belief that we can do it. As Walt Disney said, "If you can dream it, you can do it." We dream about improving the quality of life for children and families through a community system planning approach that focuses on changing public schools so that they can better serve all of the children, all of the time. We believe in Future School.

Key Terms and Concepts

Interagency collaboration. The development of an action agenda among a variety of agencies that involves cooperation in attaining common aims and objectives.

Local reputation. The generally held image of an organization, agency, or place as to its major strengths and weaknesses.

Means-ends problems. The confusion of means for ends, in which something other than the "results" of education systems are made the basis of needs assessment.

Mission statement. A declaration of the essence of a system's purpose.

Needs assessment. A formal process for determining the gaps between desired and actual conditions and the means for resolving them.

Shewhart cycle. A generic planning process developed by Dr. Frank Shewhart; steps involved in the cycle are plan, do, study, and act.

References

Coleman, J. S. (1987). Families and schools. *Educational Researcher, 16*(6), 32-38.

Comer, J. P. (1980). *School power.* New York: Free Press.

Cook, W. J., Jr. (1990). *Strategic planning for American schools.* Cambridge, MA: Cambridge Management Group.

Deming, W. E. (1993). *The new economics for industry, government, education.* Cambridge, MA: MIT Center for Advanced Engineering Study.

Florida Department of Education. (1992). *Needs assessment for Florida schools: School improvement team materials.* Tallahassee: Author.

Hodgkinson, H. (1993). American education: The good, the bad, and the task. *Phi Delta Kappan, 74,* 619-623.

Kaufman, R. (1992). *Strategic planning plus: An organizational guide* (rev. ed.). Newbury Park, CA: Sage.

Kozol, J. (1991). *Savage inequalities: Children in American schools*. New York: Crown.

National Center for Educational Statistics. (1992). *The condition of education*. Washington, DC: U.S. Department of Education.

Perelman, L. J. (1992). *School's out: Hyperlearning, the new technology, and the end of education*. New York: William Morrow.

Sarason, S. (1990). *The predictable failure of school reform*. San Francisco: Jossey-Bass.

Shanker, A. (1992). The crisis in education and the limits of the traditional model of schooling. In J. Lane & E. Epps (Eds.), *Restructuring the schools: Problems and prospects*. Berkeley, CA: McCutchan.

Steffy, B. (1993). *Kentucky educational reform: Lessons for America*. Lancaster, PA: Technomic.

✧ 5 ✧

Educational Futures
in Collaborative Systems

The American system of education is obsolete. Generally, it functions well when the work of the school is supported, assisted, and reinforced by the home and/or when both the primary and secondary clients of the educational system are involved. When this support is not present, the schools often fail. Because the number of American families willing to provide or capable of providing this support is diminishing, there is a strong need for the present system to be replaced with some form of an educational future in which an entire community takes responsibility for the growth and development of its children.

A World-Class Educational Future

Figure 5.1 shows how schools, parent, students, and the community currently interrelate to produce high school graduates who meet world-class standards. In this example, the needs of a few primary and secondary clients of the system are being met. The constancy of purpose for this small group of students is for them to attain admission to the best colleges and universities in the world, to complete undergraduate and advanced degrees, and to become fully functioning citizens of the 21st century.

The reality of continuous improvement is evident in the school program as more of the latest technology becomes available for these students and the school curriculum is updated to reflect the most current knowledge base. Students in this category own calculators, computers, and a variety of software. Frequently, they are more proficient with computer programs than their teachers. Great care is taken by parents, educators, students, and the community to assume that the educational program offered by the school is continually improving to prepare these students to be adult leaders.

The concepts of constancy of purpose and continuous improvement work so well for this population that parents of these students frequently become vocal opponents of changing the system to meet the needs of other students. These parents like the competition of standardized tests because they want to know how well their children are doing in comparison with other children. They apply great pressure to their children to make sure that they do well in school. These parents are often leaders in the community, and they know how to work the political system to attain and preserve what they want for their children.

The challenge in creating Future School is to provide all children with this kind of educational experience, which assures success. Now, only for the students achieving world-class standards do all four components contribute to the successful attainment of high levels of student competence. Expectations for this attainment begin early in the student's life, when the young child is introduced to a home environment where books are valued and the child frequently sits in the loving arms of a parent and is read to. From these early experiences, the child makes a connection between books and being held. During these early reading episodes, the attention of the adult is totally on the child. There is the warmth of close physical contact and an opportunity for quiet, calm conversation. The experience is so pleasurable for the child that frequently it becomes part of the bedtime ritual or a preface to nap time. When a visitor comes to the home and the child determines that he or she is a "safe" adult, the child will often bring books to the visitor to read. Grandparents are often targets for this activity.

During the early formative years, critical ingredients for meeting world-class standards are being met by the home environment. These include good health and nutrition habits, disciplined schedules, order, routine, travel, varied social experiences, and a strong em-

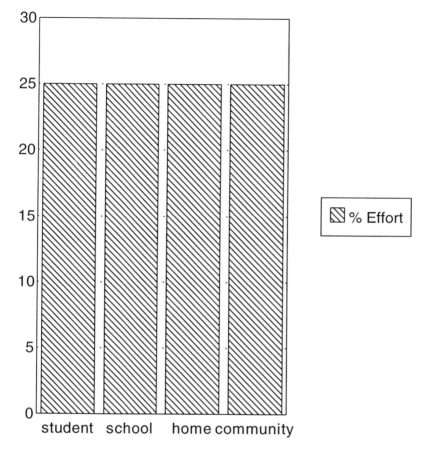

Figure 5.1. High School Graduates Meeting World-Class Standards

phasis on school readiness skills. In households where both parents work outside the home, the parents take great care to select day care that supplements and promotes these same practices.

Thanks to legally mandated car seats, the children in such families learn to accept long periods of time strapped into moving vehicles. They learn to occupy their time by looking out the window, thinking, or observing. While they are quietly observing and listening, they are learning. The physical environment that they know from their car seats exceeds that of their immediate homes or neighborhoods.

The concept of the world is different for these children than it is for children who do not travel this way.

Within their homes, these children have the opportunity to see adults continuing to learn, whether by reading daily newspapers or studying manuals for new computer programs. There are trips to museums and zoos, where the natural curiosity of adults and children is engaged.

By the time these children reach the schoolhouse door, they are prepared for success in school. The school accepts them and establishes partnerships with their parents. The children recognize that the expectations of the school are reinforced by the home, and the children naturally want to please both. A school-home partnership is a formidable force for a young student. At the first sign of difficulty, a parent will initiate a conference with the teacher to understand the problem and seek whatever help is necessary to resolve the difficulty. If a tutor is needed, one is secured. If a personality conflict exists with the teacher, the parent agitates for a change. If the school is poor, the family may move. Because the parents understand the political system in which the school operates, they use it to ensure that their child gets the appropriate learning environment. The school rewards the student with stars, grades, honor-role status, and induction into the gifted and talented program. By the time the child reaches third grade, patterns of behavior for the student, school, and parents have established educational capacity for attaining world-class standards.

The community supports the student by offering programs such as Boy Scouts, Girl Scouts, Little League, Junior Achievement, and others designed to support the values of the family, business, and government. As the student matures, there are summer employment opportunities in city government, or law offices, or city parks. For these children, success is based on the collaborative and supportive efforts of all four segments—the home, school, student, and community.

Schools That Currently Fail

Figure 5.2 depicts the imbalance among these four variables when the present system fails. For these students the school system

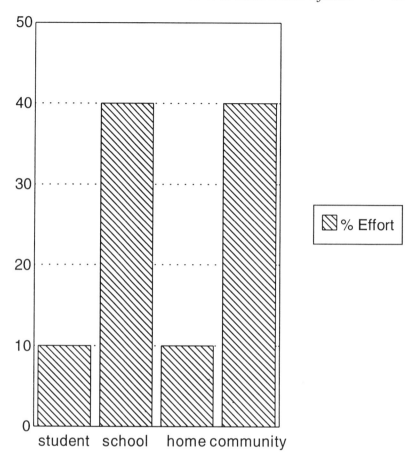

Figure 5.2. Present System Failure

becomes one that creates barriers to pride and joy of workmanship. It is a system filled with fear: fear of retention, fear of making failing grades, fear of ridicule, and fear of not being accepted. In this example, the effort put forward by the home and the student is greatly reduced and the effort put forth by the school and the community is substantially expanded. For each, the effort is of a decidedly different nature. Some would argue that this is needed for the home and the student to change. We would argue that such efforts are not realistic, given the demographic, economic, and political prospects for this country that we have seen during our professional lifetimes.

For many reasons, the home life of the child born into circumstances that traditionally lead to school failure are different from the circumstances that produce a student who achieves world-class standards. For this child, the home is not enriched with books. The ritual of reading stories is less likely to occur. The learned bedtime ritual may include more time for watching the latest sex-laden, violent TV show than anything else. Money is often a problem, as is day care. A friendly neighbor or relative may agree to watch the child during the day, negating the opportunity to learn socialization and school-readiness skills from a formal day care program. The amount of travel is limited, as is the opportunity for the child to explore the world through visits to zoos or museums. This is not to say that such children are not loved—they certainly are. Parents in such families often want the very best for their children, but they are simply unable to provide it (Epstein, 1987; Lightfoot, 1978; Lindle & Boyd, 1991).

When these children enter formal, traditional schooling, they are at a disadvantage. Although most of them enter the kindergarten door as bright-eyed, bushy-tailed potential achievers, they quickly learn that they are victims of the system. Any seasoned, astute educator can walk around a third-grade classroom and identify at least one child who has already given up. This child faces nine more years of failure if he or she decides to stay in the system. Most do not. By middle school they have become discipline problems. By high school age they could be substance abusers, dropouts, status offenders, teenage parents, or all of the above.

The schools inadvertently create barriers through special programs such as summer school, Chapter I, or special education services, in addition to providing an army of guidance counselors, social workers, and psychologists. All of these professionals and programs, with good intent, tend to take children out of the mainstream and label them, and the label is not a complimentary one. Few of these children, once labeled, ever attain world-class standards. As these students progress through the system, they become more and more withdrawn, contributing less and less effort until finally they reach an unspoken pact with their teachers: If you don't bug me, I won't bug you. This situation perpetuates a cruel waste of human potential, one this nation can no longer tolerate.

The community agencies interfacing with these children and their families during this time are not usually the Boy Scouts and the Girl Scouts. They tend to be the welfare system, health services, and the justice system. Again, with the very best intent, these services are often uncoordinated and lack continuity over time; at best, they serve as a Band-Aid, not a cure.

The result is that the schools keep doing what they have been doing, the community keeps doing what it has been doing, and the system keeps producing more of what the system has been producing. The solution lies in changing the system, expanding the system to include all four components as subparts of the new system we call Future School.

Future School

Location

Today, approximately 70% of mothers work outside the home. Many leave home more than an hour before they need to leave for work in order to drop their children off at local day care centers. School buses later pick the children up from day care and take them to school. The process is reversed at the end of the day, when mothers and fathers stop to pick up their children on the way home from work.

Currently, more and more businesses are providing on-site day care facilities. Parents like this option because it eliminates the extra stop at the day care center and it offers parents the opportunity to have lunch with their children or simply to visit in the classroom. Children like it because they know their parents are nearby. Because many large companies already have paramedical staff employed on-site, the services offered at their day care centers often exceed those offered by private child-care providers.

Adding facilities to house satellite school sites in addition to day care is also becoming more common. Part of the plan for the world's largest shopping mall in Minneapolis, Minnesota, included provisions for a school to be housed in the mall. Dade County, Florida, operates satellite schools in several off-school sites.

Given this trend, and the needs of working parents, it is clear that the enrollment boundaries for schools will change. They will become more fluid and flexible. Voucher systems may emerge in which the state and federal money supporting the education of a child follows the child, not because one school is necessarily "better" than another school, but because of the convenience for working parents. There may be a time when approval of plant location in a community is linked to providing physical space for day care, schools, and social services. It has been a common practice in the past for home developers to provide space for school construction. Given the changing needs of families, it may be appropriate for employers as well as home developers to provide this space.

There is also a trend for athletic programs to become more community based rather than school based. With the current stress on personal physical fitness, many schools have eliminated competitive sports at the middle school level. At the same time, there has been an increase in community soccer programs, Little League, and a variety of other athletic opportunities. Almost every community has one or a number of athletic clubs in addition to the local YMCA/YWCA. In many families, all members participate in some form of physical fitness. All of this may lead to a redefinition of where and when students participate in athletic and physical fitness programs.

As students become more involved in community service and business internships, they will spend less and less time in the physical environment of the traditional high school. It may become more important to have high schools situated closer to the centers for these opportunities. In the future, high schools may be located in industrial parks rather than on the outskirts of town. "Tech-prep" programs are burgeoning as students begin their technical training while in high school and complete the training at the local community college. In the future, students may be spending more time on the community college campus and less in the high school because of access to expensive, sophisticated equipment. It is no longer fiscally prudent for states to duplicate equipment in community colleges and high schools.

The same is true for business training centers. Many large companies support staff and facilities to conduct training. If an industrial park included space for education facilities, they could serve all of the businesses in the park. Because workers employed by the businesses in the park would fill all types of positions, the chances are they would live in all kinds of communities. If the school enrollment boundaries matched the place of employment rather than the place of residence, we might be able to balance the student population served by the school more equitably.

Transportation costs would drop dramatically, because fewer students would travel to school on school buses. School attendance rates would undoubtedly increase with students traveling to and from school with their parents. School-parent communication patterns would improve, because parents would be close by if there was a need for a conference or if they simply wanted to visit a classroom.

The possibilities are limitless. Perhaps the industrial park would be the site of the local library or YMCA. Perhaps citizens could rent school classrooms after regular school hours and use them to offer music or art lessons. The adult education component of the school could be expanded to accommodate students in after-school programs.

This could lead to the elimination of mass inspection, because everyone would become familiar with the programs and services offered by the larger community. It would foster the constant improvement of the system of production and service and break down barriers among agencies/groups/schools as each facet of the community became more integrated into the work of the others.

Who Teaches? Who Learns?

In Future School, everyone teaches and everyone learns. Teacher certification as we know it today will disappear, because it will become obsolete. Students will have access to the best teachers in the world. Adults in the classrooms may be volunteers, paraprofessionals, aides, citizen experts, or teachers. Every classroom will be connected electronically with the world through two-way interactive video, satellite, and computers.

Teachers will be trained to design and access information for students. They will not be expected to know or deliver all instruction. No one individual could possibly be expected to be current in all knowledge related to a given field. However, that knowledge will be available to students. Teachers will receive generic certification as opposed to specific certification in a category or a content area such as physics or French. Students studying physics will be able to choose their instructors from a library of videos of the best instructors in the world. Or, if they prefer, they can be instructed live, via satellite. This practice is already being implemented through distance learning channels for rural and small schools.

Fear will be driven out of the learning place—fear of failure for the student or the teacher. Because teachers will be trained to link appropriate instructional strategies with a student's learning style, the joy of learning will be returned to schools. That joy is evident in the eyes and behavior of our youngest students today, those in kindergarten and prekindergarten. It will be evident in the eyes and behavior of all of our students in the future. In fact, the term *student* could appropriately be connected to anyone of any age who is learning.

Human beings love to learn. Our present system of education has stifled that love, but it has not destroyed it. No one has ever been able to connect success in school with learning how to drive a car or becoming a contributing member of society. Any visit to a 20-year class reunion will reinforce the truth of this statement. Yet learning how to drive a car and being a contributing member of society both require learning. So the problem that causes schools to fail with nearly 40% of students is not a problem in the ability of children to learn. In fact, many of these same students are able to demonstrate that they can read, write, and compute by passing the GED exam by the time they are 28 years old. So the problem is not a learning problem, but a schooling problem. It is not a problem of willing students—it is a system problem, primarily an educational system problem.

Global Literacy

What does it mean to be globally literate? By all predictions, students currently enrolled in school will be expected to function effectively in a worldwide community. By today's standards, many are having difficulty functioning effectively in neighborhood communities or their own families. Yet the expectation for the future is clear. How will we possibly achieve it?

In some respects, it may be easier than we think. If we are able to produce high school graduates who can function effectively in a global economy, that means they will be able to accept diversity; respect people with different customs, clothes, and cultures; communicate in a variety of languages with or without the support of technology; understand the interdependence of countries, cultures, and continents; understand the customs, values, and norms of many people; and feel confident in unfamiliar surroundings. If we are able to provide our future high school graduates with these kinds of skills, they will surely be able to function effectively in their communities and their families.

Achieving these skills requires a basic belief in oneself, boundless curiosity, the ability to work in diverse situations, and a general acceptance of others. Belief in oneself comes from being confident of one's ability to handle situations successfully, whether in school or out. Most 2-year-old children have a deep and abiding belief in themselves. They can control their environment rather skillfully and can successfully achieve most of their goals. Their learning is continuous, and they take great delight in it. However, in the artificial world of the school, with targets, exhortations, and slogans, children learn to doubt their ability. Although they understand how important school is, they also understand very early in the formal schooling process that they have little control over their success.

Many children are very much like the "willing workers" in Deming's (1993a, pp. 158-175) famous red bead experiment. In this experiment, the workers are supposed to fill a paddle with white beads. However, the box of beads has some red ones mixed with the white ones. The workers are not permitted to take the red ones out of the box. Rather, they must insert their paddles and pull them out. Each time, the number of red beads on their paddles is counted. The worker with the fewest red beads is rewarded. The worker with the largest number of red beads is fired. In this system, the worker has no control. Clearly, failure at this task is not the fault of the worker, but of the system. We would argue that, for many children in school, lack of success is not the result of the children's incompetence, but of the incompetence of the system. The system must be changed to remove the barriers that prevent all children from developing belief in themselves.

When people believe in themselves they are more willing to take risks. Part of being curious is being willing to take risks. Curiosity about what the world looks like from the top of a tree means taking the risk of climbing the tree. The desire to learn is closely aligned with curiosity. If you are curious about how a computer word-processing program works, you are likely to learn how to use it. Most new learning that adults do is not undertaken because they have to, but because they are curious and want to.

New learning does not have to be easy for it to maintain a student's curiosity. In fact, it should be difficult enough to cause students to work, but not so difficult, or so laden with sanctions if they are not successful, to cause them to develop a fear of failure. Young boys learning how to play basketball will spend hours practicing, make many mistakes, and yet keep trying. Students learning to play chess spend hours of intense concentration. Students learning to win at a new video game keep practicing until they are successful, and then they look for a more difficult game to conquer. Learning comes with sustained challenges.

We must pace instruction to capitalize on the natural curiosity of children. Interagency collaboration can help remove the barriers of health problems, family dysfunction, and poverty. However, the schools are responsible for removing the barriers related to instructional delivery systems that diminish the natural curiosity of children.

The Student

Before day care, working mothers, computers, television, microwaves, jet travel, calculators, and CNN's live coverage of war, our factory model of schooling appeared to be satisfactory, at least for the average American family. Of course, there were those who dropped out of school, but the economy seemed to absorb them into low-paying service jobs or factory positions. Schools were satisfactory places to learn about new things, socialize with friends, and establish oneself as a person in one's own right, apart from one's family. In addition, schools provided a form of day care for children and young adults under the age of 17.

In those days, students learned about Native American Indians by studying racially biased social studies material during elementary school. Students at the junior high level were taught that government leaders were moral, honest, and true. High school students learned that the United States was a world leader and that our form of government was the best that could be attained. Generally, students were tolerant of teachers who lectured and of assessment mechanisms that measured students' abilities to memorize facts.

Today's students are far more sophisticated, worldly, and street-smart. By the time they enter kindergarten, with the help of Big Bird, Barney, and day care, they can count to 10, recognize basic colors and shapes, say or sing their ABCs, know how to get along in small groups, and understand that the world is made up of all kinds of places and all kinds of people. They have watched hundreds of hours of television, viewing fantasy, war, festivals, famines, sex, crime, anger, suffering, celebrations, and a world beyond themselves every day.

By the time they enter middle school, they know how to use microwave ovens, VCRs, and computers, all of which they probably learned at home. With cable TV they have access to programming that includes Nickelodeon, movie channels such as HBO and Showtime, CNN, travel channels, and MTV. If they want to learn about Lincoln's Gettysburg Address, they can link into an electronic encyclopedia and view a reenactment of the event. If they want to improve their math skills, they can load a computer program to provide self-paced instruction.

By the time they are in high school, if they want to socialize with friends they can get in their cars and meet at the local gas station/convenience market or the nearest mall. Adolescents beyond the age of 14 are relatively self-sufficient, mobile, and quite proficient at judging the expertise of educators. Though they are not intimidated by adults, they seek relationships with adults that are built on strong mutual trust and respect. Unfortunately for many of our current students in high school, they do not often form these relationships with their teachers. Every child needs and deserves a positive adult role model, a nourishing adult mentor, and a faithful adult friend. If opportunities to form these relationships cannot be found at school or in the home, then it is the responsibility of the community to provide them.

Tomorrow's students will have more access to global knowledge and convenient sources of entertainment. On the other hand, as the world becomes smaller, opportunities for intimate, supportive, guiding relationships also diminish. Future students will be stimulated by universal information, but the question remains, Who will guide them, love them, and support them as they learn to handle these universal conveniences? Who will invest the social capital to provide educational capacity?

The Curriculum

The curriculum for Future School will be less and more: less content and more application, less lecture and more discovery, less time in traditional classrooms and more application in the community, less prescribed at the state or district level, and more selection discretion for teachers and students. Acquiring skills and an understanding of concepts will become more important than specific content knowledge. The ability to function effectively in group situations to solve problems and complete tasks will become as important as the ability to work effectively alone to solve problems and complete tasks. Demonstrating the ability to think critically, to conceptualize solutions, and to support and defend positions both verbally and in writing will replace the need to be able to regurgitate facts. The ability to apply knowledge to the solution of real-life problems will become the measure of academic growth.

Traditional content-area instruction that takes place in 45- or 50-minute periods will disappear as we move toward greater integration of instruction. Departmentalization as we know it today will become obsolete, because our present system leads to the creation of barriers within the school and barriers between the school and the community.

High school departments in the future may be organized around Howard Gardner's (1983) concept of multiple intelligences. These departments may include business leaders, parents, and citizens with expertise in specific areas. The high school classroom will

extend into the community, and students will have major responsibility for selecting learning experiences to achieve specified outcomes. Letter grades and Carnegie units as measures of what students know and are able to do will be replaced by exhibitions,
portfolio reviews, and performances, all of which will be reviewed
by teachers, parents, business leaders, citizens, and the community.

The concepts of data-based decision making and continuous
progress will become the foundation for planning individual student curricula. Periodic benchmarks for student achievement will
be established as guidelines for curricular design, and students will
be expected to achieve these benchmarks. Benchmarks will be held
constant, but everything else will be customized for the student,
such as instructional materials, learning time, subject matter, instructional strategies, and source of instruction. Benchmarks em-
body constancy of purpose as school, community, business, and
government work in collaboration to enable each student to achieve
these benchmarks.

Assessment strategies used to document attainment of benchmarks will be made public, so that everyone understands what tasks
must be performed and how they will be judged. Student attainment of benchmarks will become a measure of how well the system
is functioning. If students fail to meet benchmarks, the system will
be scrutinized to correct problems within the system, school, community, business, or government that may have caused the deficiency. As we noted previously, Deming (1993b) maintains that 85% of
the problems within systems as they stand today are system problems,
and not willing worker problems. In Future School, this will not be
the case.

Benchmarks

Benchmarks should be established for each level of Future School.
If the buildings are organized into K-4, 5-8, and 9-12 schools, then
the benchmark and exit performance demonstrations should be
specified for 4, 8, and 12; currently, the National Assessment of
Educational Progress is designed to assess these levels. It is extreme-
ly important that when students leave one school to attend the next

level there is documentation of the fact that they have attained the benchmarks specified for the sending school. The benchmarks for fourth grade might include the following:

- Read at grade level.
- Compute using the four basic operations.
- Use basic skills to think critically and solve problems.
- Use the writing process to create, revise, edit, and publish written work.
- Use technology to access information and record written work.
- Work effectively in group situations and independently.
- Understand basic terms and concepts associated with the physical and social sciences, arts and humanities, and practical living.
- Assume responsibility, ownership, and accountability for continuous progress.

The benchmarks for eighth grade might include these:

- Understand the interrelated nature of a community and apply basic skills to the solution of concrete, real community problems and be able to justify solutions in writing and through oral presentations.
- Identify research problems, state questions, and conduct investigations involving current local, state, national, and international issues.
- Demonstrate an understanding of the interrelated nature of the global community and the similarities and differences among cultures.
- Become a self-directed learner.
- Read, write, and compute at grade level.
- Be able to converse in three languages other than English at levels sufficient for travel and survival.
- Demonstrate knowledge of the fundamental concepts undergirding the major content areas and use this knowledge to describe issues, solve problems, and forecast future trends.

- Demonstrate a knowledge of the historical development of people over time and the events that shaped that development.
- Work effectively alone and in groups.
- Work in collaboration with significant adults, family, and community and business leaders to design a secondary program to meet exit criteria from high school.

The benchmarks for 12th graders receiving high school diplomas could include the following:

- Demonstrate skills necessary to make a successful transition to work, the military, or postsecondary education.
- Demonstrate a comprehensive knowledge base in the fine arts, humanities, and social and physical sciences.
- Demonstrate proficiency in the use of advanced technological equipment.
- Demonstrate physical and mental well-being.
- Demonstrate the ability to express solutions to complex problems orally and in writing.
- Demonstrate the ability to understand and work with diverse groups in a variety of problem-centered situations to achieve consensus and solve problems.
- Be confident of one's skills and abilities and optimistic about what one can achieve in the future.
- Be able to travel, work, and communicate effectively in the world community.

Certainly the lists presented here are not complete. In keeping with the concept of continuous improvement, they would be constantly evolving to reflect new competencies students must acquire. It should be noted that the lists above are purposefully not content specific. Because our knowledge base is constantly expanding, there is no one body of knowledge all students must have. At the instant such a body is defined, it becomes obsolete and violates the fundamental principles of TQE.

Interagency/Group Collaboration
to Create Future School

In Figure 5.3 we present our vision for the profile of effort required for students without strong support from home, but with enlarging social capital through the increase of educational capacity by the entire community. There are only three categories in this model. The role of the student and the role of the school have been expanded even beyond the expectations for students currently achieving world-class standards. The most dramatic difference in this model is that the role of the family has been expanded to include other significant adults and has been blended with the community role. In this model the differentiation between primary client and secondary client has become blurred. Depending on the need, the community may take on a primary client role too.

The trick here is to create social capital and expand educational capacity by forming a federation of support for the child that emulates, to the greatest extent possible, the support base provided by the parents of academically achieving students. Through parenting classes provided during prenatal care, mothers can be taught about the importance of reading to their children. Books can be provided as gifts from the community. Perhaps a Welcome Wagon service can be initiated for newborns. If parents cannot read to their children, retired teachers could go into the homes and read to them. Or intergenerational reading programs could be established in which parents are taught to read as well as how to read to their children. Many retired seniors are perfectly able and willing to serve as day care helpers for children. The churches could take a more proactive role in providing day care services also. Preschool programs for 4-year-olds are becoming increasingly popular across the country as a mechanism to provide youngsters from disadvantaged backgrounds an opportunity to "catch up." Why wait until a deficiency exists? The senior citizen population, in most communities, is the one that is growing by the largest percentages. Many seniors live alone and are lonely. The development of community programs to utilize their skills would benefit both the seniors and the community's children. The objective is to mobilize the human resources within the community to provide all preschool children with some of the same

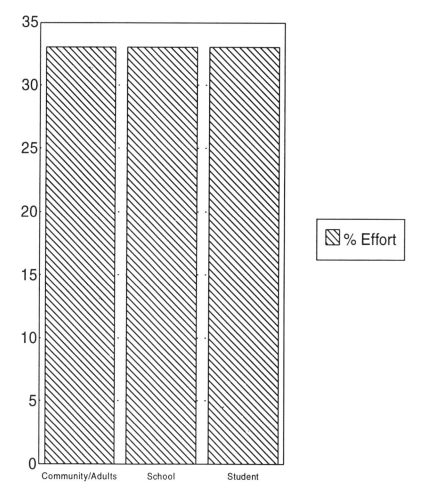

Figure 5.3. Future School

enriching and empowering experiences provided by supportive parents. In this model, other significant adults within the community take on the role of the parent.

We can hear the cries of critics who say that it is not the job of the community to do this. Well, it seems to us that we already take on this job when children reach school age. With the present system, it is not working. These children turn into dropouts or graduates who are functionally illiterate. They often become status offenders and end up incarcerated or part of the welfare system. We believe that cycle can be broken.

Noted educational researcher Ron Edmonds has been credited with the saying, "We can, whenever we choose, successfully teach all children whose schooling is of interest to us. We already know more than we need to do that. Whether or not we do it must finally depend on how we feel about the fact that we haven't so far." W. Edwards Deming believes in creating systems where there are no losers, where everyone wins. Future School is such a system.

Key Terms and Concepts

Continuous improvement. The idea that change is a process with no end, not a transition from one position to another.

Global literacy. The capability of the student to understand the function of responsibility in a community of "world-class" standards; implies an understanding of cultural pluralism.

Positive adult role model. An adult whom children can emulate and who empowers them as learners and future responsible adults.

World-class educational future. An ideal condition toward which an agency or system strives in the interest of global literacy.

References

Deming, W. E. (1993a). *The new economics for industry, government, education.* Cambridge: MIT Center for Advanced Engineering Study.

Deming, W. E. (1993b, May 11-14). Remarks made at a conference on quality assurance, Dallas, TX.

Epstein, J. L. (1987). Parent involvement: What research says to administrators. *Education and Urban Society, 19,* 119-136.

Gardner, H. (1983). *Frames of mind.* New York: Basic Books.

Lightfoot, S. L. (1978). *Worlds apart: Families and schools.* New York: Basic Books.

Lindle, J. C., & Boyd, W. L. (1991). Parents, professionalism, and partnership in school-community relations. *International Journal of Educational Research, 15,* 323-337.

Planning and Troubleshooting Guide

Planning

Strategic Planning

Team Building

TQE Applied to Business, Community, and Government